1979

S0-BBT-286

The edge is what I have" :

3 0301 00087013 5

Till the gossamer thread you fling catch somewhere,
O my soul.
Walt Whitman

"The Edge Is What I Have"

Theodore Roethke and After

Harry Williams

Lewisburg
Bucknell University Press
London: Associated University Presses

LIBRARY
College of St. Francis
JOLIET, ILL.

© 1977 by Associated University Presses, Inc.

Associated University Presses, Inc.
Cranbury, New Jersey 08512

Associated University Presses
Magdalen House
136-148 Tooley Street
London SE1 2TT, England

Library of Congress Cataloging in Publication Data

Williams, Harry.
  "The edge is what I have".

                Bibliography: p.
                Includes index.
    1. Roethke, Theodore, 1908-1963—Criticism and
interpretation.   2. Roethke, Theodore, 1908-1963
—Influence.   I. Title.
PS3535.039Z93   811'.5'4   75-5146
ISBN 0-8387-1706-3

PRINTED IN THE UNITED STATES OF AMERICA

811.54
R719w

Contents

8 6 3 19

Preface

The plan of this book is quite simple: to proceed from what has already been written about Theodore Roethke—the criticism and biography—critically assess the poetry in terms of the long poems, and to use that assessment as a lens to focus upon the writings of five contemporary poets who acknowledge Roethke's achievement. One might immediately object to an *influence* study, and rightly, I think, when such a study is narrow to the point of artificiality in its zeal to prove a connection. But influence can mean more than the mere borrowing or stealing of ideas and images. Even T. S. Eliot—no slouch when it came to stealth—used the term freely, despite his earlier derision of it, when he discussed the merits of Poe, Whitman, and Hopkins. Eliot, of course, was interested in influence because it involves comparisons, and comparisons are illuminating. By comparing the five poets I have chosen here with Roethke, I would hope that some light is shed upon the literary community Roethke helped to establish, a community in which the modern problem of identity was reevaluated and given new expression by this poets' poet. I would hope, too, that whatever errors in judgment I have made here will be set aright through the subsequent efforts of others engaged in a similar enterprise.

7

I especially want to thank Professor Marjorie Perloff whose invaluable insights brought me closer to my subject. I also wish to express my appreciation to Professors Milne Holton and John Howard for their constructive suggestions; to the editors of the Bucknell University Press for their indispensable assistance and especially to George Magee for his extra time and efforts; and to my wife Lorna, whose unfailing reaction to my incessant questions was astute as her moral support was constant.

Acknowledgments

I wish to thank the following publishers for having given me permission to quote from published works:

Doubleday & Company, Inc., for permission to quote from Theodore Roethke, "The Shape of Fire," "The Lost Son," "The Long Alley," copyright © 1947 by Theodore Roethke; "Meditations of an Old Woman," "Words for the Wind," "The Voice," copyright © 1955 by Theodore Roethke; "Open House," "The Premonition," "Mid-Country Blow," copyright © 1941 by Theodore Roethke; "In Praise of Prairie," copyright © 1937 by Theodore Roethke; "Cuttings (later)," copyright © 1948 by Theodore Roethke; "Weed Puller," copyright © 1946 by Editorial Publications, Inc.; "Frau Bauman, Frau Schmidt, and Frau Schwartze," "O, Thou Opening, O," "Old Lady's Winter Words," copyright © 1952 by Theodore Roethke; "A Field of Light," copyright © 1948 by The Tyger's Eye; "Where Knock is Open Wide," "Praise to the End!", "I Cry, Love! Love!", copyright © 1950 by Theodore Roethke; "Unfold! Unfold!", copyright © 1949 by Theodore Roethke; "The Dance," copyright © 1952 by *The Atlantic Monthly*; "They Sing, They Sing," copyright © by Theodore Roethke; "The Wraith," copyright © 1953 by Theodore Roethke;

9

"The Other," copyright © 1956 by *Botteghe Oscure*; "The Pure Fury," copyright © 1958 by Theodore Roethke; "Love's Progress," copyright © 1955 by *The New Republic*; "Memory," "The Wall," copyright © 1956 by *The Atlantic Monthly*; "The Young Girl," copyright © 1961 by Curtis Publishing Company; "In a Dark Time," copyright © 1960 by Beatrice Roethke as Administratrix to the Estate of Theodore Roethke; "The Tree, the Bird," copyright © 1961 by Beatrice Roethke as Administratrix to the Estate of Theodore Roethke; "Her Longing," "Her Time," "The Abyss," "Infirmity," copyright © 1963 by Beatrice Roethke as Administratrix to the Estate of Theodore Roethke; "Give Way, Ye Gates, The Sensualists," from the book, *The Collected Poems of Theodore Roethke*, 1966. Reprinted by permission of Doubleday & Company, Inc. and Faber and Faber Ltd. Also for permission to quote from James Dickey, *Sorties: Journals and New Essays*, copyright © 1971 by James Dickey; *The Eye-Beaters, Blood, Victory, Madness, Buckhead, and Mercy*, copyright © 1968, 1969, 1970 by James Dickey, reprinted by permission of Doubleday & Company Inc. Also for permission to quote from Ted Hughes, *Poetry Is*, "Meet My Folks," reprinted by permission of Doubleday & Co., Inc. and Faber & Faber Ltd.

Harcourt Brace Jovanovich, Inc., for permission to quote from T.S. Eliot, *Collected Poems* 1909-1962, 1963, copyright © 1936 by Harcourt Brace Jovanovich, Inc.; copyright © 1963, 1964 by T.S. Eliot. Also for the quote from "Burnt Norton" in *Four Quartets* by T.S. Eliot, copyright © 1943 by T.S. Eliot, copyright © 1971 by Esme Valerie Eliot. Reprinted by permission of Harcourt Brace Jovanovich, Inc. and Faber and Faber Ltd.

Harper & Row, Publishers, Inc., for permission to quote from Robert Bly, *The Light Around the Body, 1967*, copyright © 1967 by Robert Bly, and from, *Sleepers Joining Hands, 1972*, copyright © 1973 by Robert Bly. Reprinted by permission of Harper & Row, Publishers, Inc. Also for permission to quote from Sylvia Plath, *Ariel, 1965*, copyright © 1965 by Ted Hughes. Reprinted by permission of Harper & Row, Publishers, Inc., Olwyn Hughes, and Faber and Faber Ltd. Also for permission to quote from Ted Hughes, *Lupercal, 1960*, copyright © 1960 by Ted Hughes; *Wodwo, 1967*, copyright © 1967 by Ted Hughes; and *Crow, 1970*, copyright © 1971 by Ted Hughes. Reprinted by permission of Harper & Row, Publishers, Inc., Olwyn Hughes, and Faber and Faber Ltd.

Alfred A. Knopf, Inc., for permission to quote from Sylvia Plath, *The Colossus, 1962*, copyright © 1961 by Sylvia Plath. Reprinted by permission of Olwyn Hughes, and Faber and Faber Ltd.

Liveright Publishing Corp., for permission to quote from Hart Crane.

The Macmillan Company, for permission to quote from William Butler Yeats, *The Collected Poems of W.B. Yeats*. Reprinted by permission of A.P. Watt & Sons, London, and M.B. Yeats, Miss Anne Yeats, and Macmillan of London & Basingstoke.

New Directions Publishing Corporation, for permission to quote from Ezra Pound, "Canto 54" from the book, *The Cantos of Ezra Pound, 1948, 1965, 1971*, copyright © 1940 by Ezra Pound. Reprinted by permission of New Directions Publishing Corporation, and Faber and Faber Ltd.

Turret Books, for permission to quote from Ted Hughes, *Recklings, 1967*. Reprinted by permission from Olwyn Hughes.

University of Washington Press, for permission to quote from Ralph J. Mills, Jr., ed., *On the Poet and His Craft: Selected Prose of Theodore Roethke, 1965*, and *Selected Letters of Theodore Roethke, 1968*. Reprinted by permission of the University of Washington Press.

Viking Press, Inc., for permission to quote from D.H. Lawrence.

Wesleyan University Press, for permission to quote from Robert Bly, *Silence in the Snowy Fields, 1962*, reprinted by permission from the author. Also for permission to quote from James Dickey, *Poems 1957-1967*, 1967, reprinted by permission of Rapp and Whiting. Also for permission to quote from James Wright, *Collected Poems, 1971*. Reprinted by permission of Wesleyan University Press.

Introduction

Poets and Critics on Roethke

Throughout Theodore Roethke's middle and late career and after his death in 1963, poets have enthusiastically praised his work, while major critics have generally ignored or slighted him.[1] Not until the fifth edition of the well-known anthology, Sanders, Nelson, and Rosenthal's *The Chief Modern Poets of England and America* (1970), was Roethke included; and only recently in a collection of essays, *Profile of Theodore Roethke* (1971), the editor, William Heyen, pointed out that nine of his ten contributors were themselves poets (the single exception being Roethke's biographer, the late novelist Allan Seager), thus again reminding one that Roethke is essentially a poet's poet.

What later poets particularly admired in Roethke's work was the unusual intensity of the lyric voice, the projection of a preconscious self into the life of plants and animals, using highly original free-verse patterns that presented the speaker, the *I* in the poems, as unmasked—the poet himself asserting an oracular voice that tries to sound out archetypal themes, often probing the child-parent relation through a selective use of surrealistic imagery, that is, the "deep image." Carolyn Kizer quoted the poet himself in his role of teacher at the University of Washington (1947-63): "I teach a beat"; and she went on to underscore one of Roethke's characteristic rhythms—the end stopped, strong

13

stress trimeter line, to which the poet continually returned
throughout his career. Largely because of Roethke's presence in Seattle, she surmised, a significant number of
talented poets gathered there.[2]

If Roethke was revered for his mastery of the short line,
he was equally revered for his mastery of the long line. His
"great verbal sophistication," as Howard Nemerov describes it, manifests itself, not in the unit of the line, but in
the strophe.[3] James Wright, once a student of Roethke's,
captures this twofold lyrical quality when, in his own poetry,
he writes, praising his teacher: "And sweet Ted Roethke,/ A
canary and a bear," or elsewhere in referring to Swift's
poems: "These are the songs that Roethke told of,/ The
curious music loved by few."[4] It is this lyricism defining an
epic theme—what Stanley Kunitz calls the poet's protean
journey of transformation out of the self—that accounts for
Roethke's particular appeal and influence. For Kunitz,
Roethke's lyrical journey out of the self is a real achievement because he does not indulge his ego, and as a result he
"was the first American bardic poet since Whitman who did
not spill out in prolix and shapeless vulgarity."[5]

Leslie Fiedler sees Roethke's work as seeking out myth
and image in the privacy of dreams rather than in a decay-
ing culture. Roethke's journey is a returning, not to a lost
culture, but to the greenhouse of his youth where his father
watched over and cared for a floral culture; and it is a
return, as Fiedler perceptively describes it, "to all that is
truly subversive in the line that comes down to us from Poe
by way of *symbolisme*."[6] Delmore Schwartz, who sees Roethke
as original and important enough to be compared to Yeats
and Valéry, notes Roethke's genuine awareness of the
"abyss," the depths of the unconscious to which all romantic
poets must return for self-definition and value.[7] Because
this return to the unconscious is dangerous, courting

psychic disaster, achievement of self-renewal is at best precarious. Failure is always close at hand, yet self-renewal "is what we want: to be gathered together once more," says James Dickey, quoting from the end of Roethke's "The Long Waters." Roethke extends into modern times that Wordsworthian sense of *being*, of reunification with nature and one's self, and for this reason alone Roethke is for Dickey the greatest American poet there has ever been.[8] Perhaps C. W. Truesdale has best summed up Roethke's appeal by equating Roethke's second volume, *The Lost Son and Other Poems* (1948), to Whitman's "Song of Myself"—an extension, in fact, of Whitman's poetics, exhibiting a controlling metaphor of organic growth and a progress from darkness to light: "Most of what we call the American archetypes find themselves again in his work (in unexpected ways), and above all the sense of the land—the vast, the particular, the wasted, the utterly beautiful and the utterly exploited landscape of America, the motherland of Thoreau, Whitman, Twain, even Cooper." Truesdale does not identify the major works, as such, other than "The Lost Son" sequence of poems, but it is the theme of resurrection in that sequence that, for Truesdale, defines Roethke's appeal: "the poet is always the 'lost son' seeking a fresh birth in a new America."[9]

In reviewing Roethke's first collection of verse, *Words for the Wind* (1958), John Berryman compares Roethke with Robert Lowell; the two "possess the most powerful and original talents that have emerged during the last fifteen years." If Lowell is Latinate, formal, rhetorical, massive, historical, religious, impersonal, then Roethke is "Teutonic, irregular, colloquial, delicate, botanical and psychological, irreligious, personal"—a formidable list of comparisons, indeed, but comparisons that perhaps Roethke would have agreed with, since he had remarked at one time about

Lowell's excessive concern with formal structures, and about his lack of intuitive perception.[10] Berryman also singles out the longer poems in "The Lost Son" sequence as Roethke's largest achievement, one of the "fixed objects" in American poetry.[11]

In addition to praise, one is not surprised to find some of these poets acknowledging a direct influence. Kunitz candidly admits that Roethke had taught him a way of coping with affliction.[12] Galway Kinnell insists that no one really had any influence on his work, "until I ran across Theodore Roethke's poems."[13] In accounting for Ted Hughes's poetic power, W.E. Snodgrass sees Hughes doing the same thing as Roethke.[14]

Anne Sexton remembers "writing to Sylvia [Plath] in England after *The Colossus* came out and saying something like ' . . .if you're not careful, Sylvia, you will out-Roethke Roethke,' and she replied that I had guessed accurately and that he had been a strong influence on her work."[15]

Just what these poets saw in Roethke's work that the critics found convenient to ignore raises interesting questions that I shall try to answer throughout the ensuing pages. Why, for example, should so many critics have remained cool for so long to the romantic archetypes and lyricism that attracted the poets to Roethke in the first place? Perhaps it is the lack of a well-defined terminology for the motive and effect involved in any exchange between two or more poets—as Richard Wilbur has recently suggested in an essay on the subject of poetic influences. Wilbur reminds one that poets do borrow, steal, adapt, translate, impersonate, and parody one another, and that it is the business of other poets and also of the critics to account for this behavior. Wilbur himself discusses the beneficial effects of the Yeatsian influence on Roethke in the early fifties, an influence that Roethke literally documented in "Four for

Sir John Davies" and "The Dying Man," as well as the poem later added to the greenhouse sequence in *The Lost Son*, "Frau Bauman, Frau Schmidt, and Frau Schwartze." In fact, the trimeter line Carolyn Kizer speaks of is a product of this Yeatsian influence. Of course, an influence can become merely derivative if it is not transformed in the younger writer's imagination, for in reading any poet the reader is always put into that position where he must distinguish between what is wholly belonging to the poet—what is stolen, to use Eliot's phrase—and what is merely borrowed. Without referring to particular poems, Wilbur sees Roethke's later poetry, after the "Yeatsian poems," showing an absorption of the older writer's influence, and hence a perfection of the Roethkean voice.[16]

Although many of the major critics were silent about Roethke at mid-century and after, there were some critics who raised specific objections. In his study of modern English and American poets, *The Shaping Spirit* (London, 1958), A. Alvarez defines the "unmannered," confessional mode of the American poet who writes from a sense of his own isolation within a classless, unstructured society. Speaking about *The Lost Son* in general, Alvarez argues that Roethke failed to succeed as a confessional poet. Roethke's talent "of a kind" (of a much lower caliber than that of Lowell's or Eberhart's) is delicate and direct in its treatment of the poet's "private troubles" (Alvarez refers to only one of the greenhouse poems, "Cuttings"), but because there is no sense of embarrassment, there is offered only an immediate purity and not that "overbearing, claustrophobic intensity" that Alvarez would have. In Roethke's subsequent volume, *Praise to the End!* (1951), Alvarez sees the poet as merely exploiting his material, using his verse "as though it were an analyst's couch." Roethke's artistic identity is a matter of nonconformity and being different: "He

ends where the important writers begin, in that sense of
isolation from which they create an impersonal artistic order."

M. L. Rosenthal's first critical introduction, *The Modern
Poets* (New York, 1960), also treats Roethke as part of the
confessional school of American writing. The greenhouse
poems of *The Lost Son* volume are (contrary to Alvarez).
"embarrassedly alive," yet, "as in most of Roethke's longer
works, the dénoument does not live up to the poem's initial
demands." Generally a defender of the "new poetry," Rosenthal is severely critical of Roethke's personal manner,
"the private sensibility of a mad microcosm" that seeks unity
and wholeness that, in the case of "The Lost Son," is merely
wishful thinking. In his second study of poetry since World
War II, *The New Poets* (New York, 1967), Rosenthal reiter-
ates his position and further extends his remarks to Roethke's posthumous volume, *The Far Field* (1964), which he sees
as "often marred by verbosity, cliché, and derivativeness."
Admitting that Roethke came into his own as a poet in his
group of greenhouse poems, "that his youthful experience
around his father's greenhouse in Michigan provided just
the vivid, squirmingly uncomfortable, and concrete focus
his poetry needed to channel," that these poems enabled
him to objectify for a time his "uncontrolled, riotous
psyche," Rosenthal nevertheless objects to Roethke's seeming inability to absorb "so little of the concerns of his age
into his nerve-ends . . . so little reference direct or remote to
the incredible experiences of the age." In Roethke's hands,
then, the confessional mode is reduced to self-recharging
and self-echoing.

The charge that Roethke's poetry is outside the experiences of the age is repeated by Monroe K. Spears in his
study of modern poetry, *Dionysus and the City* (New York,
1970). Referring generally to "The Lost Son" sequence,
Spears admits that Roethke's poetry at its best has a "deep

inwardness and closeness to the Unconscious," yet because the Dionysian element is so strong, the poetry refuses to deal with "the world of normal adult experience." As a result, much of the verse tends toward incoherence and "real obscurity."

It has been demonstrated how some poets revered Roethke's lyricism, his voice of the self proclaiming a drama of the new self, but certain critics have found this preoccupation with the self too narcissistic. Discussing the nature of the modern lyric, William Pritchard looks upon Roethke as a representative figure of the "somnambulistic" poet devoid of irony and changing tone of voice. Pritchard would advance the cause of a Frost, or a Lowell—despite the singular tones of a Milton, or a Blake, as Pritchard himself admits— the cause for a lyricism that gestures between lyric impulse and the "wryly satiric."[17] These "negative" critics appear to agree on at least two points: Roethke's limited theme that makes him (embarrassed or not) merely a personal, self-conscious poet, and his lyric form or lyrical monotone. These negative criteria, however, can be turned to Roethke's account.

In his seminal essay, "The Vegetal Radicalism of Theodore Roethke" (*The Sewanee Review*, Winter 1950), Kenneth Burke offered for the first time a challenging structural approach to *The Lost Son* volume. Burke recognizes at once the symbolic importance of the greenhouse for Roethke (in Roethke's words: "A womb, a heaven-on-earth"), and from the thirteen-poem greenhouse sequence (now fourteen), he singles out that poem about the greenhouse itself, "Big Wind," as being representative of Roethke's method in all of these poems—his "intensity of *action*" whereby the poem develops from stage to stage, with the "unwinding of the trope." It is not the close description of flowers that makes these poems succeed—although this is clearly part of Roethke's intention—but the fact that Roethke can make his flowers suggest analogues to human behavior and motives quite like the figures of animals in Aesop's fables. In exploiting the floral image, even as a conceit, as Burke sees it, Roethke could develop these analogues on different levels of meaning (root, sprout, blossom), all the while amplifying his theme by a regressive withdrawing of the self ("the most occult of early experiences"). In this greenhouse world with its "peculiar balance of the natural and the artificial," there is almost a perfect symbol for that mystery that relates the individual with the social: "In hothouse flowers, you confront, enigmatically, the representation of status. By their nature, flowers contribute grace to social magic—hence, they are insignia, infused with a spirit of social ordination." In establishing Roethke's radicalism, Burke distinguishes between Eliot's aesthetic and that of Roethke's—the latter, for example, expressing an intuition of sensibilities having a minimum of ideas and a maximum of intuitions, hence a poetry of impulse rather than motive. In this way Roethke's vocabulary is shorn of the abstract—words with -ness or -ity endings—that characterize much of Eliot's poetry. Eliot meets the modern problem of identity in terms of doctrine, while Roethke grapples with that problem in opposite terms, regressing as thoroughly as he could, "even at a considerable risk, toward a language of sheer 'intuition.'" Moreover, Roethke's images become symbolically intuitive when they interchange their meanings through repetition in varying contexts; thus fish, water, flower, or girl might form a symbolic cluster by the repetition of each of these images in related contexts. In this way the images fuse their respective meanings: "They are 'fusions' if you like them, 'confusions' if you don't, and 'diffusions' when their disjunction outweighs their conjunction."

    In dealing with the longer sequences, including "The Lost Son," Burke touches on two important techniques that have come to characterize Roethke's method in all of his long poems, as shall be seen later. The first is Roethke's shifting voice, extending the *I* of the speaker into a "cosmically communicating 'voice.'" The second is the way the imagery brings into tension the concrete and the abstract by almost always invoking the notion of "edge" (also suggested by the disjunctive qualities of the truncated, and end-stopped lines): "the constant reverberations about the edges of the images give the excitement of being on the edge of Revelation (or suggest a state of vigil, the hope of getting the girl, of getting a medal, of seeing God). There is the pious awaiting of the good message—and there is response to 'the spoor that spurs.'" Burke reprinted his essay in his collection, *Language as Symbolic Action* (Berkeley, 1966), without changing it, for, as he was to say in a note appended there, "I cannot better contrive to suggest the rare, enticing danger of Roethke's verse as I felt it then, and still do."

Nothing of critical importance appeared in the decade following Burke's essay. Perhaps the publication of one notable volume of poetry (*The Lost Son*) coming seven years after Roethke's first volume, *Open House* (1941), was not enough of a production to attract serious attention. Also, the radicalism that Burke proclaimed may well have cautioned critics, for Roethke was to become more experimental (as the poems juxtaposed to Burke's essay were to show) in his next volume, *Praise to the End!*, which effectively extended "The Lost Son" sequence. Moreover, consistency was not Roethke's habit: he introduced a neo-Yeatsian mode in *The Waking* (1953) and extended it further into *Words for the Wind* (1958), all the while carrying over poems from one volume to the next. But in the sixties, especially after Roethke's death and his posthumously published *The Far Field* (1964), a number of important critics began to give this poet their attention. Arnold Stein edited a collection of essays in *Theodore Roethke: Essays on the Poetry* (Seattle, 1965), the first collection that indicates Roethke's new-found acceptance by the critical establishment. Most of the essays tend to support Roethke's growth as a poet, but because of the breakthrough made by *The Lost Son* and the radical experiments of the related poems in the *Praise to the End!* sequence, two questions naturally suggest themselves: do these two volumes—and specifically the former—constitute Roethke's achievement? Is there no growth and development in the later poetry?

Stephen Spender, W. D. Snodgrass, John Wain, and Louis Martz argue for a decline in poetic strength. Spender, for example, acknowledges Roethke's nonegotistic search of the *I* in "The Lost Son" sequence from these two volumes—hence the title of his essay, "The Objective Ego"—yet in the later poetry Roethke exhibits "the Yeatsian grand manner, he becomes the egotist who burdens the reader with his problems." A perpetual beginner, Roethke could not extend his childlike visions of organic nature into the world of society as everyone must come to know it; "he was not a free enough intellect to dominate the Yeatsian mode." Snodgrass's particularly incisive essay, "'That Anguish of Concreteness,'" similarly sees a failing in the later Yeatsian poems; but if Roethke, "who had invented the most raw and original voice of all our period," had misused the formal and elegant voice of Yeats, he had not done so with Eliot's voice (a less confining influence), which is behind the long sequence, "Meditations of an Old Woman," for here the Roethkean voice clearly emerges. In the later poems from *The Far Field*, the mystical and religious rationale and the borrowed cadences become too pervasive for Snodgrass, as does Roethke's penchant for rejecting form as he creates it in his seeking a unity with all objects. Eliot's ideas and Yeats's cadences have become models of form, "have rushed in to fill the vacuum of the father-model." Rejection of form, then, becomes itself a form, a convention, and the language then becomes weakened through slackness and "expectability." John Wain, in his essay, "The Monocle of My Sea-Faced Uncle," similarly praises "Meditations of an Old Woman," more for its originality and evocation of a genuinely feminine personality. Roethke is the only poet of the century who successfully refuses compromise between inner and outer reality by insisting on his intensity of vision, and to write about those things "that the mind apprehends only through the intuitions of the body." For these reasons *Praise to the End!* occupies a central place in the Roethkean canon. Louis Martz, on the other hand, sees Roethke's originality in terms of mind rather than bodily intuition. Applying Wallace Stevens's lines, "The poem of the mind in the act of finding/ What will suffice," to Roethke's manner, Martz reveals a meditative mode displaying a speaker/actor who "seeks himself in himself in order to discover or to construct a firm position from which he can include the universe." Roethke's meditative manner develops out of the greenhouse poems—"one of the permanent achievements of modern poetry"—and reaches its zenith in the longer sequences making up the last section of *The Lost Son*, "The Greenhouse Eden" (Martz's title), to which Roethke would return in his later poetry, but never surpass.[18]

The later poetry receives more sympathetic treatment from Ralph J. Mills, Jr., Frederick J. Hoffman, William Meredith, Denis Donoghue, and Roy Harvey Pearce. Mills's essay, "In the Way of Becoming: Roethke's Last Poems," treats the Roethkean journey as a quest for mystical illumination, a quest that alternates between contrary states within the "reflective consciousness" of the speaker—between ecstasy and despair—as in "Meditations of an Old

Woman" and "North American Sequence." However, it is not until "Sequence, Sometimes Metaphysical," constituting the last section of *The Far Field*, that Roethke reaches his peak in the process aimed toward "a union with or experience of the Divine." Unlike the freer, Whitmanesque rhythms with their breath-controlled strophes in "North American Sequence," the lyricism in "Sequence, Sometimes Metaphysical" is taut and economic, "capable of containing and concentrating immense pressures of feeling," (the two sequences exemplifying Roethke's opposing rhythmic forms). What Snodgrass sees as a weakness in this last volume, Roethke's desire to escape *all* form and shape, is precisely what Mills commends as "Roethke's mystical perceptions by striking inward steadily with little recourse to external affairs . . . approximating the instant of naked revelation."[19]

Donoghue, Meredith, and Pearce approach the poetry as an ordering of chaos, both inner and outer, private and public. Donoghue's perceptive essay, "Roethke's Broken Music," follows the Burkean example in tracing Roethke's "intuition of sensibilities" to define that ordering process. If the early poems held out the common romantic idea of the opposing self, the middle and late poems develop the sense of losing one's self at the edge of the abyss, and "the abyss is partly the frog-spawn of a blind man's ditch, partly a ditch of his [Roethke's] own contriving, partly the fate of being human in a hard time, partly the poet's weather." This is the way to innocence; the poems are intuitive directions, akin to spiritual exercises, "all the better if they are caustic, purgative, penitential. The exercises are never finished, because this is the way things are, but once they are well begun the soul can proceed; the energy released is the rage for a sustaining order." Donoghue stresses Roethke's universal appeal, insisting that he is never merely a regional or American poet. He gives two valid arguments: first, Roethke's eclectic influences (Eliot, Hopkins, Joyce, Whitman, Stevens, Yeats) preclude such labeling, and, second, Roethke's response to the parental figures (and the wife or lover in the love poems) is so vivid it engrosses all other responses that would better define a regional or local poet. In the poet's search for value and meaning there is an assumption on Roethke's part that this search is only interesting insofar as it is representative, and of no interest when it ceases to be. "Roethke set himself to work toward lucidity and order without turning himself into a case study entitled, 'The Still Complex Fate of Being an American' . . . . But," Donoghue adds, avoiding a seeming contradiction, "Roethke's way of being an American is an eminently respectable way, and part of his achievement is that he makes it available to others." It is just this availability, the nature of Roethke's influence, that is studied in the last chapter of this text.[20]

In Meredith's essay, "A Steady Storm of Correspondences: Theodore Roethke's Long Journey Out of the Self," the assertion is again encountered that the *Praise to the End!* volume is central, "an anatomy of Roethke's imagery and sensibility" in which he explores the self without egotism. Flirting with "the slow rhythm of chaos," Roethke makes knowledge felt by means of syntax and rhythm; human speech becomes instinctive, "primarily involuntary, an animal cry." Pearce, on the other hand, is concerned with what he calls "the power of sympathy" in the later poetry. Roethke "could not understand the compulsive twentieth-century quest for identity via the route of alienation"; yet there *is* alienation in the poetry, but it is often associated with violence and only by means of sympathy is that violence transformed into power, thus, "alienation into identification." The argument of Roethke's "North American Sequence" is "to unify and make all of a piece, the world which has invaded the poet, so as to allow him to invade it." In this way the poet comes "to comprehend the full range of

8 6 3 1 9

LIBRARY
College of St. Francis
JOLIET, ILL.

the other, that chain of being which moves from the minimal to God."[21] Finally, there is Hoffman's incisive essay, "Theodore Roethke: The Poetic Shape of Death," stressing Roethke's dual language, the metaphysical and the natural. It is Roethke's particular success—unparalled in modern American poetry—to have kept the two so well balanced, so reciprocal. Similar to Louis Martz, Hoffman regards Roethke's work as a poetry of the mind. The mind entering itself is Roethke's "steady concern," and to effect this metaphysical extension of himself he had to go beyond the greenhouse and the "papa principle" in *The Lost Son*, even though a sense of return was always imminent. The Roethkean persona looks into death's possibilities, he sees dying as "continual becoming," a knowledge "of growth as a move toward mortality," which finds its best expression in "Meditations of an Old Woman." In *The Far Field* Roethke develops metaphors of transcendence, that is, the will to transcend the particularity of the temporal process in order to define the self, and it is in the late poem, "In a Dark Time," that Roethke resolves "the mazes caused by life and the problems created by the expectation of death."

As excellent as many of these essays are, they are inevitably concerned with only the general qualities of Roethke's poetry. Within the compass of a brief essay, one can offer little structural criticism of specific poems, although what is provided is a needed emphasis on the Roethkean theme—the journey out of the self.

Aside from Burke's criticism of "The Lost Son," the earliest work done on a specific poem is Hugh Staples's essay, "The Rose in the Sea-Wind: A Reading of Theodore Roethke's 'North American Sequence'" (*American Literature*, May 1964). Stapes traces the sequence's structural pattern, describing the first poem of the sequence as an overture introducing the thematic imagery that will operate as leitmotifs throughout the sequence. The middle four poems alternate between sets of opposing images, earth and water, for example, or light (fire) and darkness; thus "Meditation at Oyster River" is dominated by water imagery, "Journey to the Interior" by earth imagery, the cycle repeating itself with the next two poems, "The Long Waters" and "The Far Field." A final version is then offered in the last poem, "The Rose," which presents the rose as the symbol of form, and here the sequence reconciles and resolves all the thematic images of the previous poems, gathering them together as a final achievement of unity.

Staples's method is both explicative and critical, and it may be that together with Burke he inspired further explication, the most notable example being the only book-length study so far, Karl Malkoff's *Theodore Roethke: An Introduction to the Poetry* (New York, 1966).[22] Malkoff's thoughtful explication of the entire range of Roethke's poetry falls short of any critical assessment of the poet's style and structure, but it does serve a most useful purpose in explicating key themes from a psychoanalytical point of view. The longer poems from the last of *The Lost Son*, for example, show Roethke's "adept manipulation of a subterranean, Freudian universe," and in so doing are original for contemporary poetry at that time. In viewing the poetry from psychological perspectives, Malkoff stresses the poet's personal sense of guilt—sexual in "The Lost Son," and in the form of a personal mysticism trying to take over in "Meditations of an Old Woman" and "North American Sequence." In assuming that guilt operates the controlling theme, Malkoff is forced to account for what appears to be Roethke's ambivalence (between the personal and the impersonal) in conceptualizing terms of myth and legend, and by using Freud and Jung, or other writers of consequence. As a result, Malkoff sometimes belies an impatience with Roethke's poetic strategies, as in the case of "Four for Sir John Davies": "The victory over the powers of darkness and nonbeing . . . is at best tentative; and this sets the pattern for the bulk of Roethke's remaining poetry, which is characterized by a tormenting vacillation between hope and despair rather than any consistent point of view."

Extending Staples's structural approach and enlarging upon Malkoff's basic explications, a few good studies of individual poems have appeared over the past several years. William Heyen in his essay, "Theodore Roethke's Minimals" (*Minnesota Review*, 1968), shows how Roethke's random selection of minimals (worms, mice, dogs, children, crows, and the like) is not meant to offer a development or hierarchy, as in a great chain of being, but rather is made to support the poet's varying moods. Most of the images represent stages of becoming and being, as in "Meditations of an Old Woman" where the woman's alternate moods of elation and despair are reflected in the way she interprets the bird and its song during the entire sequence. Heyen's criticism favors a mystical approach to the poetry, and a year later one finds him writing toward that end in a second essay, "The Divine Abyss: Theodore Roethke's Mysticism" (*Texas Studies in Language and Literature*, Winter 1969).[23] Heyen concentrates on "The Abyss" from *The Far Field* in order to develop Malkoff's assertion that Roethke was quite familiar with Evelyn Underhill's *Mysticism*. That the poem's five-part structure corresponds to Underhill's outline of five phases of mysticism (awakening of self; purification of self; illumination; the dark night of the soul; union) is somewhat weakened by Heyen's admission that the fourth phase, the dark night of the soul, finds little correspondence in the poem. Yet the poem is the "prototypical" mystical poem, and the mystical journey it suggests is the very essence of many of Roethke's later poems in *Words for the Wind* and *The Far Field*.

Another essay of a more explicatory mode than Heyen's is James McMichael's "The Poetry of Theodore Roethke"

(*The Southern Review*, Winter 1969). McMichael again emphasizes the Roethkean predicament—the journey out of the self, and particularly its relationship to the meaning of God for Roethke, the desire to find one's God: "I have emphasized," says McMichael, "that the *sine qua non* of Roethke's journey out of the self is his commitment to the mindless part of God's creation." Woman and animals are the mediators of this "mindless part" because they are closer to the "soil." In "North American Sequence," however, woman is precluded from the hierarchy of mediators of this "his most complete definition" of the journey out of the self. McMichael follows Staples's treatment of leitmotifs in the sequence as a hierarchy of elements within an earth-air-water framework. The final poem of the sequence is an ambitious attempt to define the paradoxical relationship between self and other and achieve as much resolution as possible. The rose, as symbol, is outside the hierarchy of mediators that has been at work in the preceding five poems; yet the value of the rose is somehow related to the transiency of this hierarchy, and the fact that this commitment might sink to nothingness leaves the poet (and the reader) with an acute sense of man's central dilemma.

Reworking Burke's ideas about Roethke's "intuition of sensibilities," Jerome Mazzaro develops a linguistic/psychological metaphor to explicate a sampling of the poetry in his essay, "Theodore Roethke and the Failures of Language" (*Modern Poetry Studies*, July 1970). Again, Mazzaro underscores the success of Roethke's intuitively directed language because it is symbolically informed. But something is lost in the process, and that is language's failure to communicate cognitively when it is intended to function symbolically. Roethke exemplifies that peculiar energy that depth psychologists claim an American culture creates, an energy "emanating from the tensions produced by the distance between the high level of her conscious

culture and an unmeditated unconscious primitive landscape." Mazzaro's account for the unintelligibility of some
of the poetry, particularly in *Praise to the End!*, amounts to an
apology for the poet: "for complete interaction, his [the
reader's] sensitivity to symbolic language must equal the
poet's."

As if to exemplify Mazzaro's pronouncement about
psychic parity between reader and poet, John Vernon offers his explication of "The Lost Son" sequence in *Praise to
the End!* in his essay, "Theodore Roethke's *Praise to the End!*
Poems" (*The Iowa Review*, Fall 1971). In attempting to account for the entire "Lost Son" sequence (not to be confused with the greenhouse sequence of an equal number of
poems), Vernon discusses the first few poems, particularly
the opening poem, "Where Knock is Open Wide," giving
very little attention to the central poem, "The Lost Son"
(until Vernon's essay very little, if nothing, of critical significance had ever been done with the "nonsense poems" making up part of this sequence). Vernon sees the dynamism of
the child's world depicted in these poems; it is a synaesthetic
world in which the imagery is predominantly sexual and
parental. Father, mother, and self define a trinitarian identity that is always fluid because it is always holding in tension
notions of separateness and mergence, of time and
timelessness, of presence and absence.

In writing about the rise of a sacramental visionary mode
in literature replacing the "supernaturalist figuralism" of
the past, Nathan A. Scott, Jr., in his recent book, *The Wild
Prayer of Longing: Poetry and the Sacred* (New Haven, 1971),
devotes a chapter to Roethke as the exemplary poet of the
sacred. Scott refers to Roethke's Blakean remark that everything that lives is holy, and he sees Roethke's sacramental
verse as peculiarly American, promoting a sense of awe or
wonder in the tradition of Whitman, Twain, Melville, or
Thoreau. Roethke's praise of the small, calling upon snails,

weeds, birds, and the like, keeps him away from the mystical, the supernatural, the "Supreme Fictions," even "God." Despite the fact that Roethke's sacramental vision is primarily limited to the nonhuman world, he deserves to be included "among the major poets using the English language in this century" because he knew "the very essence of the sacramental principle—namely, that nothing may be a sacrament unless everything is."

Brendan Galvin's "Theodore Roethke's Proverbs" (*Concerning Poetry*, Spring 1972) has given some needed attention to the proverbial, axiomatic quality of Roethke's poetry. A poem is seen as an aggregate of lines, of proverbs, separately recorded at various times in the notebooks, and it is the proverb that, for Roethke, was a way of ordering experience, "strategies" to cope with the problem of identity and to "induce his courageous plunges into the mire of the preconscious, and his subsequent returns."

What can be concluded from this criticism? Perhaps only two or three agreed-upon assertions at most—namely, that Roethke's controlling theme is the journey out of the self, that his lyric mode draws upon those of Yeats and Whitman, and that "The Lost Son" and the related poems forming "The Lost Son" sequence are central to his poetry. The rest is controversy—his mysticism, his symbolism, his range, his objectivism, his influence. Why this controversy persists (a healthy sign in itself) may be due to the absence of any thorough treatment of the poetry itself, that is, a critical assessment of more than one poem or sequence that would help establish the Roethkean mode of identity without reducing the poems to Freudian puzzles as Malkoff does. There is, of course, Burke's incisive but brief treatment of "The Lost Son," but nothing more of any consequence, except perhaps Staples's analysis of a decade ago of that other longer sequence of poems, "North American Sequence." Burke's analysis of "The Lost Son" sequence is directed to the greenhouse poems, "The Lost Son" itself receiving only selected criticism and not an extensive analysis of the entire poem. Staples's analysis of the later sequence is not only good, but also thorough and, therefore, difficult to improve upon; yet there still remains the job of tying this last sequence into the earlier ones, a job that Staples could not have contemplated, focusing almost exclusively, as he did, on the single sequence itself. Allan Seager reports that the long poems making up "North American Sequence" came easily "with an unwonted confidence," that Roethke "knew what he wanted to say and he was sure of his means."[24] If this is true, accepting the centrality of "The Lost Son," the longest poem in the *Praise to The End!* sequence, then surely the one is an outgrowth of the other. There is, however, that other long sequence, "Meditations of an Old Woman," that comes between the two in time and that is quite similar in technique to the later sequence. There are, then, three long poems (the shorter of the three, "The Lost Son," is some seventy-five lines longer than the nearest contenders for length, the Yeatsian poems) that readily offer themselves for critical assessment as a group.

There are other reasons for treating these long poems as major pieces defining the Roethkean mode; for one, they exemplify in their own way that trinitarian sense of identity that John Vernon observed in the *Praise to the End!* sequence—the death of the father theme structuring the first poem, perhaps that of the mother the second (since Kunitz believes it was written immediately after the death of the poet's mother), and then the third poem finally concentrating on the mature self.[25] Second, Roethke's greenhouse world, initially explored in the fourteen-poem sequence that makes up section one of *The Lost Son*, is never absent from these long poems; in fact, the greenhouse image is significant in each poem, making the group itself a unit for that reason alone. Third, each of these poems is somehow concerned with the urban world, the city, outside the "natural" world. In an essay entitled, "On 'Identity,'" Roethke describes his principal concerns as follows: "(1) The multiplicity, the chaos of modern life; (2) the way, the means of establishing a personal identity, a self in the face of that chaos; (3) the nature of creation, that faculty of producing order out of disorder in the arts, particularly in poetry; and (4) the nature of God Himself."[26] He goes on to refer to his own poem, "Dolor," as a footnote to the inanimate sterility of the institution; "the 'order,'" says Roethke, "the trivia of the institution is, in human terms, a disorder, and as such, must be resisted" (*SP*, 20). Resistance is precisely the method these long poems use. It might be said that they resist "false" trivia (institution trivia) with what Roethke would call "true" trivia (the trivia of "natural shapes"[27]). It is the natural shapes running through these poems that contribute to their metric and thematic unity, but it is important to note the presence of an opposing "unnatural" imagery— in other words, intrusions from the city that become more pronounced, developing chronologically through these poems. The "kingdom of bang and blab" (*CP*, 54), the disjunctive and sacred world of moss, mole, and stone depicted in "The Lost Son," can become profane and deadly as, "A kingdom of stinks and sighs,/ Fetor of cockroaches, dead fish, petroleum" (*CP*, 187), in the later poem, "North American Sequence." Thus, there is money creeping into the first of these poems; there are "the self-involved" and "those who submerge themselves deliberately in trivia" (*CP*, 169) on the borders of the speaker's mind in the second poem; and there is the waste and decadence "at the edge of the raw cities" (*CP*, 187) in the background of the third poem.

It is not usual to stress the social aspect of Roethke's poetry; indeed his ostensible neglect of the social theme has caused critics to assume that his range is limited, even as

Robert Lowell seemed to do in a rather glib remark for *The Paris Review* (1961): "The things he knows about I feel I know nothing about, flowers and so on"—although Lowell drops glibness for reverence in his poem, "For Theodore Roethke." Roethke's apparent dearth of societal referents in his poetry, however, is really no reason to assume a lack of concern for "the incredible experiences of the age"; on the contrary, his concern can be said to condition and inspire the poetry.

Finally, Roethke's poetry has a tragic dimension so far ignored by all who have written about him. Burke alludes to it when he describes Roethke's verse as having that "rare, enticing danger" about it; and Donoghue, as well, when he speaks about the loss of self as "partly the fate of being human in a hard time," that Roethke's poems, in the middle and late period, are spiritual exercises, a way toward innocence, "never finished" in their "rage for a sustaining order." I am reminded of Yeats's remarks, for he saw the tragic dimension as a controlling form in all artistic expression: "Tragic art, passionate art, the drowner of dykes, the confounder of understanding, moves us to reverie, by alluring us almost to the intensity of trance,"[28] and it is this trancelike condition that Roethke leads one to and away from in these major pieces, "for the nobleness of the arts"—to continue with Yeats's words—"is in the mingling of contraries, the extremity of sorrow, the extremity of joy, perfection of personality, the perfection of its surrender, overflowing turbulent energy, and marmorean stillness."[29] Above all, it is this perfection of personality *and* the perfection of its surrender that Roethke accomplishes in these poems.

Joyce Carol Oates has admirably restated the problem of tragedy in modern times, and I have accepted her assumptions about the nature of tragedy—namely, that the art of tragedy grows out of a break between self and community; that at its base is fear; that although actual human life may in large part be valueless ("the multiplicity, the chaos of modern life"), tragedy asserts itself as a valuable and unique human passion, "risking loss of self in an attempt to realize self"; that if the death of God means the death of tragedy, "then a redefinition of God in terms of the furthest reaches of man's hallucinations can provide us with a new basis for tragedy."[30] Because Roethke's three longest poems are themselves an expression, among other things, of this search for God (" . . . the nature of God Himself")—a redefinition of God really—they share in the search, as well, for a tragic form.

It is the tragic form inherent in these three poems that perhaps in some way defines Roethke's appeal to later poets. What Staples calls "a dimension curiously suggestive of the epic," in referring to "North American Sequence," might be Roethke's assertion of a tragic form in addition to the appeal of his deep or intuitive imagery and his verbal rhythms, especially in an age of tragic failure, an age more of pathos and nihilism. Certainly, the controversy over the essence of tragedy is healthfully active today,[31] and that Roethke should address this controversy through his art is a testament to his appeal.

In the following three chapters I shall take up, respectively, each of these three long poems in terms of the ideas discussed so far, and in the final two chapters the question of Roethke's influence in terms of the themes and lyrical qualities of the poetry discussed as well as in the poetry of some major contemporary poets. For this purpose I have chosen James Wright and Robert Bly as representative together of one facet of the Roethkean mode of experience;

James Dickey by himself representing another vision of Roethke; and Sylvia Plath and Ted Hughes representing yet another.

It would not be wrong to suppose that many contemporary poets were reacting against the studied ironies and tensions in much of the poetry of Eliot, Stevens, and Auden—perhaps Frost and some of Lowell (and one thinks, too, of Tate and Ransom)—that these poets took a second look at Roethke's romantic stamp that bore the impressions of Wordsworth, Whitman, and Yeats. What they found— the profundity of the lyric forms in the greenhouse poems and the remarkable sequences that followed—proved to have enormous appeal for them; here again was a new voice.

Notes

1. Despite Babette Deutsch's critical survey, *"The Poetry in Our Time: A Critical Survey of Poetry in the English Speaking World, 1900 to 1960* (Garden City, New York: Doubleday, 1963), which favorably refers to Roethke (pp. 197-200), the following significant surveys are silent about Roethke: Irvin Ehrenpreis, et al., eds., *American Poetry: Stratford-Upon-Avon Studies 7* (New York: St. Martin's Press, 1965); Stephen Stepanchev, *American Poetry Since 1945: A Critical Survey* (New York: Harper & Row, 1965); Ian Hamilton, *A Poetry Chronicle: Essays and Reviews* (London: Faber and Faber, 1973). Among the more significant conceptual studies of modern poetry, the following are silent: Sister M. Bernetta Quinn, *The Metamorphic Tradition in Modern Poetry* (New Brunswick, New Jersey: Rutgers University Press, 1955); Richard M. Ludwig, ed., *Aspects of American Poetry* (Columbus, Ohio: Ohio State University Press, 1962); Allen Tate, ed., *Six American Poets: From Emily Dickinson to the Present: An Introduction* (Minneapolis: University of Minnesota Press, 1964); J. Hills Miller, *Poets of Reality: Six Twentieth-Century Writers* (Cambridge, Massachusetts: Harvard University Press, 1965): L.S. Dembo, *Conceptions of Reality in Modern American Poetry* (Berkeley, California: University of California Press, 1966); William T. Noon, *Poetry and Prayer* (New Brunswick, New Jersey: Rutgers University Press, 1967); A. Kingsley Weatherhead, *The Edge of the Image: William Carlos Williams, Marianne Moore, and Some Other Poets* (Seattle: University of Washington Press, 1967); Martin Dodsworth, ed., *The Survival of Poetry: A Contemporary Survey* (London: Faber and Faber, 1970); Harold Bloom, *The Ringers in the Tower: Studies in Romantic Tradition* (Chicago: University of Chicago Press, 1971).

2. "Poetry: School of the Pacific Northwest," *New Republic* 135 (16 July 1956): 18-19.

3. *Poetry and Fiction: Essays* (New Brunswick, New Jersey: Rutgers University Press, 1963), p. 136.

4. *Collected Poems* (Middletown, Connecticut: Wesleyan University Press, 1971), pp. 146, 194.

5. "Roethke: Poet of Transformations", *New Republic* 152 (23 (January 1965): 23.

6. "A Kind of Solution: The Situation of Poetry Now," *Kenyon Review* 26 (Winter 1964): 63.

7. "The Cunning and the Craft of the Unconscious and the Preconscious," *Poetry* 94 (June 1959): 203-205.

8. "The Greatest American Poet," *Atlantic* 222 (November 1968): 53-58.

9. "Theodore Roethke and the Landscape of American Poetry," *Minnesota Review* 8 (1968): 351, 352.

10. *Selected Letters of Theodore Roethke*, ed. Ralph J. Mills, Jr. (Seattle: University of Washington Press, 1968), p. 134.

11. "From the Middle and Senior Generations," *American Scholar*, 28 (Summer 1959): 384.

12. "'Imagine Wrestling With an Angel': An Interview with Stanley Kunitz," *Salmagundi*, no. 22-23 (Spring/Summer 1973), p. 79.

13. "To the Roots: An Interview with Galway Kinnell," *Salmagundi*, no. 22-23 (Spring/Summer 1973), pp. 212, 213.

14. "W.D. Snodgrass: An Interview," *Salmagundi*, no. 22-23 (Spring/Summer 1973), p. 154.

15. "The Barfly Ought to Sing," in *The Art of Sylvia Plath*, ed. Charles Newman (Bloomington, Indiana: Indiana University Press, 1970), p. 178.

16. "Poetry's Debt to Poetry," *Hudson Review* 26 (Summer 1973): 278-80.

17. "Wildness of Logic in Modern Lyric," in *Forms of Lyric*, ed. Reuben A. Brower (New York: Columbia University Press, 1970), pp. 127-51. An opposing view to Pritchard's is offered by Donald Wesling's essay appearing in the same volume: "The Inevitable Ear: Freedom and Necessity in Lyric Form, Wordsworth and After," pp. 103-126. Wesling uses Roethke (along with Wordsworth and Whitman) to exemplify a lyricism that is discursive and descriptive; poets of this mode employ "successfully the fluid yet weighty medium of an innovating metric. In conceiving of the mind as in large measure self-destroying, but also in large measure self-creating, the psychology and prosody of the inevitable ear are at one. The tendency toward the dissolution of personal identity and the weakening of poetic shape will always exist in such a scheme, but as a risk which imposes a responsibility" (p. 125).

18. Martz's essay also appears as the ninth chapter in his study, *The Poem of the Mind: Essays on Poetry / English and American* (New York: Oxford University Press, 1966).

19. "In the Way of Becoming: Roethke's Last Poems," in *Theodore Roethke: Essays on the Poetry*, ed. Arnold Stein (Seattle: University of Washington Press,

1965), pp. 115-35. Related essays by Mills are: *Theodore Roethke*, University of Minnesota Pamphlets on American Writers, no. 30 (Minneapolis: University of Minnesota Press, 1963); "Theodore Roethke: The Lyric of the Self," in *Poets in Progress: Critical Prefaces to Ten Contemporary American Poets*, ed. Edward B. Hungerford (Evanston, Illinois: Northwestern University Press, 1962), pp. 3-24; the third chapter in his *Contemporary American Poetry* (New York: Random House, 1965), pp. 48-71.

20. Donoghue's essay appears as the eighth chapter in his study, *Connoisseurs of Chaos: Ideas of Order in Modern American Poetry* (New York: Macmillan, 1965).

21. Pearce's essay appears as the eleventh chapter in his study, *Historicism Once More: Problems and Occasions for the American Scholar* (Princeton, New Jersey: Princeton University Press, 1969), pp. 294-326.

22. Since the present book has gone to the publisher, there has appeared a second book-length study, Richard A. Blessing's *Theodore Roethke's Dynamic Vision* (Bloomington, Indiana: Indiana University Press, 1974), which is not so much a critical analysis or study as it is an overview of all the poetry, attempting to underscore Roethke's aesthetic of motion, the Heraclitean flux that shapes his vision.

23. Heyen's essay also appears in his edition of *Profile of Theodore Roethke* (Columbus, Ohio: Charles E. Merrill Co., 1971), pp. 19-46. Also appearing in this volume are the following essays that I have previously reviewed in the text: Schwartz's "Cunning and Craft," pp. 64-66; Kunitz's "Poet of Transformations," pp. 67-77; Burke's "Vegetal Radicalism," pp. 19-46; McMichael's "Poetry of Roethke," pp. 78-95; and Mazzaro's "Roethke and the Failures of Language," pp. 47-64.

24. *The Glass House: The Life of Theodore Roethke* (New York: McGraw-Hill Co., 1968), p. 252.

25. "Poet of Transformations," p. 26.

26. *On the Poet and His Craft: Selected Prose of Theodore Roethke*, ed. Ralph J. Mills, Jr. (Seattle: University of Washington Press, 1965), p. 19. Subsequent quotations of Roethke's prose from this volume will be parenthetically designated in the text by *SP* and page number.

27. *The Collected Poems of Theodore Roethke* (Garden City, New York: Doubleday, 1966), p. 166. Subsequent quotations of the poetry from this volume will be parenthetically designated in the text by *CP* and page number. In the case of detailed discussions of particular poems, references to quoted material are considered redundant and will not be given.

28. *Essays and Introductions* (New York: Collier Books, 1968), p. 245.

29. *Essays and Introductions*, p. 255.

30. *The Edge of Impossibility: Tragic Forms in Literature* (Greenwich, Connecticut: Fawcett, 1973), pp. 8-12.

31. For a thorough treatment of the subject of tragedy with its modern ramifications, *see* Geoffrey Brereton, *Principles of Tragedy: A Rational Examination of the Tragic Concept in Life and Literature* (Coral Gables, Florida: University of Miami Press, 1968).

"The Edge Is What I Have"

1

A Quest for Shape: "The Lost Son"

Or slip like water slippery towards its ends,
As foxes, stoats, and wolves, and prairie dogs.
                                        D. H. Lawrence

Roethke was fifteen when his father finally succumbed to a slow, cancerous death; a profound shock for any boy that age learning to identify with his father as one of the first steps toward self-recognition. To be suddenly deprived of this means of perspective is literally to be lost. Where does one go, and to whom does one turn when the family house is suddenly fatherless? That "empty house" (*CP*, 53) and the symbolic journey the son takes in search of the father are the subjects of "The Lost Son"; restoring the parent to the empty house is the son's way of going forward toward identity. The argument of the poem involves a twofold development defined in terms of father and son. It is the house image in the poem that symbolizes the father, in the full sense of the term, as a place of hierarchal concern, the patriarchal seat; and it is the journey theme, that is, the

41

journey away from house and father that symbolizes the
son; the return, of course, brings father and son together,
not in the house, but the greenhouse. In terms of identity, it
is the self versus the nonself, the other that is symbolized by
the field; the house with all its social ramifications vies with
the field with all its vegetal and animal ramifications. In this
way the Roethkean identity ranges from a false sense of self
(empty house) to a true one (greenhouse). The journey and
the house, then, are the two motifs structuring the poem as
they echo the house/field equation from their vantage
point.

In an oft-quoted passage from "Open Letter," Roethke
describes his method in "The Lost Son" as follows: "I be-
lieve that to go forward as a spiritual man it is necessary first
to go back. Any history of the psyche (or allegorical journey)
is bound to be a succession of experiences, similar yet dis-
similar. There is a perpetual slipping-back, then a going-
forward; but there is *some* 'progress'" (*SP* 39). It is this cyclic
form of progress that Roethke adhered to as a spiritual
theme throughout his literary career, referring to it directly
in "Meditations of an Old Woman" (*CP*, 158) and in "North
American Sequence" (*CP*, 193, 199). Its roots are in English
romantic poetry where the circuitous journey, as M. H.
Abrams describes it, is an essential feature.[1] The pattern
can be found particularly in the romantic lyric, where often
there is a return to the beginning of the journey but with an
intervening procession of awareness or consciousness that
renders the final stages of the journey significantly more
human and more integrated than the subhuman and frag-
mented existence that marked the protagonist's early stages
of the journey.

Elsewhere in Roethke's "Open Letter," he speaks briefly
of the beginning stages of his journey in "The Lost Son" and
other poems from *Praise to the End!*: "Some of these pieces,

then, begin in the mire; as if man is no more than a shape writhing from the old rock. This may be due, in part, to the Michigan from which I come. Sometimes one gets the feeling that not even the animals have been there before; but the marsh, the mire, the Void, is always there, immediate and terrifying. It is a splendid place for schooling the spirit. It is America" (*SP*, 40). These lines should put one on notice about the extent of Roethke's journey in "The Lost Son," that he is not so much taken up with completing or finishing a journey toward some end, but that he is a writhing shape within the "void" or the terrifying deeps of the unconscious, a beginning of spirit out of "the old rock."

It seems to have been Roethke's express intention to place "The Lost Son" squarely in the middle (the seventh poem) of a thirteen-poem sequence in *Praise to the End!* (1951), because he preserves this sequence (adding only a fourteenth poem) in the two subsequent volumes, *The Waking* (1953) and *Words for the Wind* (1958). In its first appearance as a collected poem in *The Lost Son and Other Poems*, only three of the poems in the *Praise to the End!* sequence appeared with it. The greater number of the remaining poems in that first volume make up the "Greenhouse poems," poems in free verse with little of the surrealistic quality of *Praise to the End!*, and, perhaps for that reason, easier to associate with "The Lost Son," which, for Louis L. Martz, "they echo and complete."[2] But the greenhouse, Roethke's symbol "for the whole of life, a womb, a heaven-on-earth" (*SP*, 39), is not absent from the supporting poems in *Praise to the End!*; it is never mentioned by name, as it is in the central poem, "The Lost Son," but it is referred to indirectly throughout the sequence. In fact, the house image is the key image, explaining or lending significance to "this struggle for spiritual identity," where "disassociation often precedes a new state of clarity" (*SP*, 41). The image, in effect, becomes symbol and operates in what Roethke has described as "a kind of psychic shorthand" (*SP*, 42) throughout the volume. Take, for example, the first poem in the sequence, "Where Knock is Open Wide"; the poem ends by relating God, father, and house:

> One father is enough.
>
> Maybe God has a house.
> But not here.
>
> (*CP*, 74)

The stage is set for this house to eventually become realized as green, for one father not to be enough ("A son has many fathers," *CP*, 98), and for God to be here ("God, give me a near," *CP*, 73). The house image finally becomes a "dreary shed" (*CP*, 92) in the last of the thirteen-poem sequence, a "hutch" for reason and grubby schoolboys, but during the course of the sequence it has been transformed into a hat (*CP*, 75), a cage (*CP*, 77), a cave (*CP*, 82), a nest (*CP*, 93), even a "horse barn" (*CP*, 59), and, of course, into a greenhouse in the central poem. These changing aspects of the "house" with its various tenants from the vegetal, human, and animal worlds (mothers, fathers, cats, mice, and roses, for example) shape the history of Roethke's prenatal psyche.

As a symbol, Roethke's house-greenhouse is especially effective because it embraces both house and field.[3] "A house for wisdom; a field for revelation" (*CP*, 90), says Roethke in "Unfold! Unfold!", anticipating the range from *Open House* to *The Far Field*, and, as well, his metaphorical range for man's identity. Within the symbolic realm of the house, the significance of Roethke's creatures, "all small shapes," becomes evident; they, like Roethke, are both domesticated and wild; they pass through the house-greenhouse; they are its symbols and the history of his true self:

> Sing, sing, you symbols! All simple creatures,
> All small shapes, willow shy,
> In the obscure haze, sing!

(CP, 90)

It is not my purpose, however, to analyze the entire *Praise to the End!* sequence, as John Vernon has recently attempted.[4] Some of the poems, or portions thereof, are opaque to analysis, taken up with the idea of psychic regression by means of the child's irrational expressions of his surroundings, expressions that Roethke abandoned after this volume. At any rate, Malkoff lists the main themes running through the sequence, such as birth, death, separation from father and God, sexual confusion and guilt, and, I would add, fear of self, of others.[5] It is true that the poems become clearer with successive readings; in Roethke's use, hands, for example, are undoubtedly symbols of guilt, as they are for Homer Simpson in Nathanael West's *The Day of the Locust* (1939), and it is only through comparison of the separate occurrences of the image that the symbolism emerges. However, much of the imagery in these poems is focused, or I should say *re*focused, in "The Lost Son," particularly the controlling image—the house.

"This is my hard time," says the speaker, the lost son, in the opening section or movement appropriately entitled, "The Flight." This voice is Roethke's acknowledging the earlier soundings of the Roethkean voice in *Open House* ("Death Piece," "The Adamant," "Prognosis," "No Bird," "The Unextinguished," and "Against Disaster," to name a few that "cry aloud" to "stop the lying mouth," *CP*, 3):

At Woodlawn I heard the dead cry:
I was lulled by the slamming of iron,
A slow drip over stones,
Toads brooding wells.
All the leaves stuck out their tongues;
I shook the softening chalk of my bones,
Saying,
Snail, snail, glister me forward,
Bird, soft-sigh me home,
Worm, be with me.
This is my hard time.

The preponderance of nasals and laterals mixes freely with voiced and voiceless spirants, giving the rhythm a viscous movement, "glister me forward," but with a few alveolar stops to check the ease of movement. Significantly, these stops throw the first and last lines into relief, "dead cry," and "hard times." The varying line lengths up to the single-stress line, "Saying," are arbitrary and contribute to a shifting sense of confusion on the part of the speaker; he is alone and frightened, alienated from nature ("the leaves stuck out their tongues") unlike the toads who are in sympathy with their surroundings, "brooding wells." The speaker's isolation is perhaps best visualized by the slow drip over stones; one can almost identify the speaker here with the single drop, the self-enclosed nodule that waits to become a part of something else. A stasis is reached, then, with his "Saying"; perhaps the speaker is learning from the toads' "brooding" *how* to speak, for in the remaining lines a sense of order comes into play with the orderly decreasing of line lengths (seven to five to four syllables) to the confidently uttered final sentence. And this last statement is credible because it emerges from the experience itself.

But why is the speaker at Woodlawn; why a cemetery? There is an earlier poem from *Open House*, "On the Road to

Woodlawn," that is obviously relevant and should give a sharper perspective to the speaker's predicament. The last line of that earlier poem describes a dead one about whose funeral the speaker is reminiscing: "I miss the polished brass, the powerful black horses" and "I miss the pallbearers momentously taking their places." This poem is no elegy, certainly not in the conventional sense as is Roethke's "Elegy for Jane," and I think it would be misleading to limit interest to either the identity of the dead one or to the grief and guilt of the speaker. Except for the last line, the poem is given over to the description of a highly formal occasion—yet the speaker misses it. He is aware of the attendant, crass commercialism, yet he is victim to it because it surrounds an important personal event in his life from which he can not escape, or better, he can not resolve in his mind. There is grief over the dead one, and there is a confusion of guilt and fear arising out of the contemptuous description of the funeral, but if the speaker is a lost son he can not have a poetic identity, he is not entitled to it because of a death in the family. Roethke's lost son must transform the father, as well as himself, into a symbolic figure, and, of course, this is what "The Lost Son" tries to do.

It is the confusion one finds in "On the Road to Woodlawn" that explains the speaker's need for "flight" in the opening of "The Lost Son." Not on the road to Woodlawn, the road over which society passes, but in and at Woodlawn is where the speaker begins his search—in the direction of sensibility with the dead and with the primitive, subhuman forms of life. At this early frightened stage of search there is no communion for the speaker. "Nothing nibbled my line,/ Not even the minnows came," says the speaker in the next stanza. The *I* is dropped, minimizing the self almost to extinction within the preconscious: "fished in an old wound,/ The soft pond of repose," no doubt a metaphor for the unconscious ("The deep stream remembers:/ Once I was a pond," *CP*, 80). This second stanza has already provided a shift of sense in its own right, for it does not try to identify the cemetery of the preceding stanza with the unconscious, but rather with the nonhuman animal world of motion and direction that is not the stasis of unconsciousness, as Roethke's pond metaphor suggests. Roethke's choice of "old wound" is adept because it relays his feelings about the unconscious, "the Void," as a source of pain and fear (". . . immediate and terrifying").

In the third stanza Roethke introduces his central symbol, the house (each of the five sections of the poem recites this symbol), an "empty house," and in this case a metaphor, as well, of the unconscious suggested in the preceding stanza:[6]

> Sat in an empty house
> Watching shadows crawl,
> Scratching.
> There was one fly.

The synesthetic "Scratching" effectively magnifies the separateness and concomitant anguish of the speaker, having escaped from the horrors of a human world to the isolation of an empty house in need of a father. Here the speaker is literally empty minded; he is the fishless pond, the empty, fatherless house from which he pleads for some kind of direction, "Voice come out of the silence./ Say something."

Although the house imagery is continued in the next two stanzas, and an appeal is made for an answer to appear "in the form of a spider/ Or moth beating the curtain" (small forms of life), an answer of sorts does come in the seventh stanza from the world of the cemetery, from the "dark hollows," the "moon" and the "salt." But the answer in no way contributes to the speaker's identity; rather, each of these natural phenomena merely suggests to the speaker an aspect of itself: wind for the hollows, the back of an eel (pure image here) for the moon, and the sea for the salt. From these comparisons, the speaker's identity then begins to emerge for the first time in the form of self-assessment, self-criticism really:

> Your tears are not enough praise,
> You will find no comfort here
> In the Kingdom of bang and blab.

For the most part this is a negative way of establishing identity, forced out of frustration, which *is* some progress. However, there is a slipping black into anonymity in the next, the eighth, stanza and throughout the remainder of the first section. What is presented here is a kind of disembodied speech as the action picks up with an increasing variety in line length. A hunt is underway; it is a quest for shape, for some sense of definition:

> Hunting along the river.
> Down among the rubbish, the bug-riddled foliage,
> By the muddy pond-edge, by the bog-holes,
> By the shrunken lake, hunting, in the heat of summer.

Roethke provides a catalogue of places here, which he will develop much further and to greater advantage in establishing his real or true self in "North American Sequence." By surrounding the speaker with other identities, Roethke is almost surely cultivating the rhythmic, the ritual of cataloguing that so often appears in Whitman. Alliteration and assonance account for the rhythm, although it should be noted that there is a three-stress line in the background on which play Roethke's alliterative and assonantal sound patterns. For example, it is the phrases that scan as three-stress lines, regardless of Roethke's doubling up of these phrases (lines) to form a six-stress line, sometimes truncated ("By the muddy pond-edge, by the bog holes"). These double-length lines, or the long Roethkean lines, as they might be called, create a sustained rhythm here as elsewhere ("Up over the viaduct I came, to the snakes and sticks of another winter,/ A two-legged dog hunting a new horizon of howls," *CP*, 65). The hunt is thematic throughout "The Lost Son" sequence, and it is almost always an anxious pursuit, closely identified with the "fearful ignorance" (*CP*, 171) of the child speaker unable to gain a perspective on himself, knowing only impulse:

> I've played with the fishes
> Among the unwrinkling ferns
> In the wake of a ship of wind;
> But now the instant ages,
> And my thought hunts another body.
> I'm sad with the little owls.
>
> (*CP*, 80)

This expression of it is typical, I think; the animistic urge is never sated because at the moment of direct identification (beyond the realm of metaphor) there is resistance to identity: "the instant ages,/ And now my thought hunts another body" (*CP*, 80). This is one way, of course, that Roethke can keep "the spirit spare" (*CP*, 3), if one can relate spirit to thought.

In the final four stanzas of "The Flight," the speaker with his disembodied voice leaves one hunting for something bigger than the shape of a rat, yet less than a leg, but sleek as an otter with wide, webby toes. With a heavy use of synecdoche, Roethke succeeds in suggesting the image of a fetus.

Again, Roethke writes a kind of ritualistic cataloguing that leaves the reader with the sense of rhythm as reality, and the fluid imagery describing these animals and parts of animals becomes the rhythm of change and flow that their watery, embryonic surroundings suggest.

The all-important question arises, then, "Could it come in the house/ On the tips of its toes?" Can this animal-spirit come into the empty house of the speaker's mind? After raising the rhetorical question, Roethke ends this first section with a water image. Water is memory ("The deep stream remembers"), and the hunt must involve a probing of his memory. "Remember-Water" (*CP*, 59).

In the next section, "The Pit," the speaker gets his nibble by means of alternately indented lines shifting the questions and answers within the womb-house ("I feel the slime of a wet nest"):

> Where do the roots go?
>   Look down under the leaves.
> Who put the moss there?
>   These stones have been here too long.
> Who stunned the dirt into noise?
>   Ask the mole, he knows.
> I feel the slime of a wet nest.
>   Beware Mother Mildew.
> Nibble again, fish nerves.

The rhythms are slow and hesitant as they sound a dialogue with the self building up to a stasis—as in the opening stanza of the poem. "Who stunned the dirt into noise?" merits a rhetorical aside, "Ask the mole" that counterpoints what the speaker can feel, the slime, and that is all one should expect, since any animistic identification would be specious, if Roethke here is faithful, as he is, to his speaker's condition.

The speaker can also utter, "Beware Mother Mildew," without defeating the sense, because this warning against the processes of aging, of discoloring, is an announcement of the speaker, of the incipient identity who will oppose these effects. It is also a warning for the mother figure, since she will be physically weakened in the cause of the speaker's nourishment. Kenneth Burke has noted the grammatical shift to the first person in the last three lines, terminating, in effect, the questions and answers posed in the first six lines. These grammatical shifts, says Burke, "keep one from noting that the stanza is in essence but a series of similarly disposed images."[7] But this grammatical shift, I think, is not so much a deception, a cover for consistent imagery, as perhaps it is a timely release for the speaker to forgo circuitous dialogue and assume a sense of self, false or otherwise ("I feel . . . beware . . . Nibble again").

The third section of the poem, "The Gibber," which denotes the bulb or swelling at the bottom of the calyx, corolla, and the like, continues the womblike surroundings of "The Pit," but, as the title connotes, alternatively, a meaningless chatter (the gibbering sounds of subhuman life) that comes into play and makes for what Roethke describes elsewhere as a "frenetic activity" (*SP*, 38).

The first three stanzas with their Dantesque imagery lead up to the crucial command, "Die." But this is not a first death as in Dylan Thomas; Roethke's speaker says, "I listened to something/ I had heard before" ("Everything has been twice," *CP*, 72), and the command to die comes from both the animate and the inanimate worlds: dogs, sun, moon, weeds, snakes, cows, briars. So again, with the stasis reached (with some forward progress) at the end of "The Pit," there is a kind of "slipping-back" the ultimate slipping back to death. "At the wood's mouth,/ By the cave's door" is where the speaker listens—womb images, again, reinforcing the house symbol of the poem and completing the parental symbol. Malkoff sees these natural objects as symbols of guilt that demand the speaker's guilt, an interpretation difficult to controvert ("Dogs of the groin" is sexual, of course, and could be a symbol of guilt). I find it difficult, however, to associate weeds, snakes, cows, briars with guilt—conceding Malkoff's identity of sun and moon with father and mother who both are "against" the speaker (it might be argued that the sun and moon are literally too large for the speaker's world of mostly diminutives).[8] To balance Malkoff's interpretation with an opposing view seems to me to be required by the poetry. These "simple creatures" need not lose their symbolic value for Roethke if, in fact, they symbolize death; that is, a knowledge of death for which the speaker, regardless of his motives, is experiencing a genuine wish. The rhythms of the third stanza show how successful Roethke is at suggesting that these creatures know something the speaker does not know (*see also*, "The Sloth," *CP*, 116):

> The weeds whined,
> The snakes cried,
> The cows and briars
> Said to me: Die.

The gibbering of these creatures, "whined" and "cried," forces itself by means of the deliberate assonance of the juxtaposed end-words of these lines to become intelligible only in the last word of the stanza. The larger assonantal rhythm linking "weeds" and "me" reinforces the effect. Also, the punctuation and the preponderance of alveolar stops slows the rhythm to a funeral step, and before the resonance of the last word is heard, the imaginary rhyme on "said" (dead) has subconsciously prepared the dénoument for the reader. In preparing for the drama of his death, the lost son assumes the role of the Christian martyr. Like Christ who was utterly isolated (only a few soldiers and some personal friends stand under the cross; even the Father himself had withdrawn his comfort), Roethke's speaker is a lone, ostracized individual surrounded only by the barest emblems of nature: weeds, briars, snakes, and cows. The father is absent here because death is the supreme personal experience; the son's psychic regression into martyrdom, however, will resurrect the father, and it is this resurrection that the fourth stanza dramatizes through the archetype of primal parents.

That the speaker's death-wish is motivated by a sexual or moral guilt seems strained. I see no reason why this death-wish should not derive from a larger source, or a less personal one than Malkoff suggests, such as the guilt anyone feels when confronted with the death of a parent, a guilt for merely being alive at the expense of death and, hence, a wish to experience death as a compensatory gesture by making some kind of metaphorical identity with it. I am not suggesting that Roethke does not raise the question of sexual guilt (note his hands symbol in "Praise to the End!"), but in "The Lost Son" this aspect of guilt is not emphasized, and surely the whole baffling subject of guilt can not be confined to just this one source.

"What a small song," says the speaker in the fourth stanza. There seems to be an inching forward, a coming out of death's realm into what appears to be a realm of fear and alienation:

> I'm cold. I'm cold all over.
>   Rub me in father and mother.
> Fear was my father, Father Fear.
> His look drained the stones.

Roethke borrows the tone and imagery from chapter thirty-eight in Job, a source he acknowledged (*SP*, 38), where the voice out of the whirlwind speaks to Job, asking him a series of rhetorical questions that serve only to frighten Job into an awareness of his own insignificance:

> Hath the rain a father? or who hath begotten the drops of dew?
> Out of whose womb came the ice? and the hoary frost of heaven, who hath gendered it?
> The waters are his as with a stone, and the face of the deep is frozen.

Roethke's language here, and elsewhere, recalls Job in its gnomic, rhetorical quality that happily defies rational analysis; the value of such language lies within the rhythms, the repetitions of sound and meaning. Anyone coming away from Job after two or three readings is hard put to discuss the syntactical and narrative meaning of that work; one is left, rather, with a sense of language as ritual. The character of Job soon gives way to the anxiety of the poet behind his character and the achievement he accomplishes by giving expression to that existential anxiety through language. In the same way, Roethke's lost son becomes his language, he identifies with the ritual of language that he (and the poet behind him) has created. A closer look at Roethke's lines reveals this sense of repetition at work ("Fear was my father, Father Fear"), that builds up the sense of a primal need to identify with parents, and his clever use of the active verb "rub" underscores the primitive that he is after. Also, Roethke plays off two opposing senses of identity, the need for and the fear of that identity by having the father figure, the primal parent, as the very source of that fear, all of which is dramatized by the father's look having the power to drain stones. These stones might be identified with the female parent overpowered by the male parent or it may be that Roethke is making an oblique sexual reference to his real adolescent state—which need not be entertained in order to understand the speaker's fear—that fear is the cause for a compensatory sexual release, onanistic or otherwise, a draining, literally, of the testicles.

It may be that this last, fourth, stanza with its long lines of varying length marks a slipping back rather than a going forward. The important point, however, is that the stanza marks a departure in rhythm from the first three stanzas, and this departure describes a fast, frenzied pace, in keeping with a state of fear. The next three stanzas (fifth, sixth, and seventh) return the rhythms of the first three stanzas, and similarly the lines lead up to a dramatic awareness on the part of the speaker. Rather than experiencing an awareness of death, the speaker talks of his waking. In the first three stanzas the speaker's experience was essentially aural, but reverts to visual and tactile ("What gliding shape/ Beckoning through halls" and "my own tongue kissed/ My lips awake"). This shift in sense to the visual might very well be a showing of some progress (Roethke proclaimed the visual as the most valuable of the senses in "Prayer," *CP*, 8) arising out of his psychic shiftings:

> From the mouths of jugs
> Perched on many shelves,
> I saw substance flowing
> That cold morning.
>
> Like a slither of eels
> That watery cheek
> As my own tongue kissed
> My lips awake.

The "halls" and "stairs" in the first of these stanzas bring back the house symbol again, and it seems that some spirit ("gliding shape") has come into the house on the tips of its toes, for it is "poised on the stair." The house symbol refocuses the sense of spirit by the suggestion of a greenhouse with the many shelves of jugs (pots). Spirit then becomes the substance flowing from the mouths of these jugs, and here Roethke is anticipating the speaker's return of his father in the next section to his greenhouse world. But before this return the embryo-speaker must be born human, and the final four stanzas of "The Gibber" take up this crucial event.

The first of these stanzas returns (slipping back?) to the fearful, frenetic rhythms of the fourth stanza. The sentient shift is one from cold to heat, and there is a shift in location as well, from caves of ice to a greenhouse (prepared by the preceding stanzas). Here "all" the windows are burning, a greenhouse where the sun could be burning in all the windows. By merely listing rhetorical questions and gnomic answers, Roethke confronts one with a most challenging stanza.

One of the more gnomic lines in this stanza is the middle line that I take to be seminal to the stanza's meaning, "Let the gestures freeze; our doom is already decided." Because a human identity is being formed within the womb-greenhouse, Roethke may be suggesting the implanting of a hereditary code within the speaker's brain, a code having a numbing effect because of its contradictory determinants of the self. Roethke dramatizes this conflict as a loss of the speaker's identity, and hence a loss of human identity and existence; man's doom is decided, thus Roethke's lament for the loser, "I want the old rage, the lash of primordial milk!/ Goodbye, goodbye, old stones, the time order is going." In this particular context I am not sure what Roethke means by "old stones," other than that the phrase is an index to an older order, "another condition" (*CP*, 99). I am reminded of Eliot's use of the phrase in "East Coker" (5):

> Not the intense moment
> Isolated, with no before and after,
> But a lifetime burning in every moment
> And not the lifetime of one man only
> But of old stones that cannot be deciphered.

Taking the hint from Eliot perhaps, Roethke has his speaker saying good-bye to an older culture, possibly a matriarchal culture ("That woman I saw in a stone—" *CP*, 123), possibly a patriarchal order if "stones" is associated with the male genitals. Certainly there is expressed a desperate desire for order, a desire for authority from a parental figure, and the accompanying tone of agony goes as far back as "Open House": "rage warps my clearest cry/ To witless agony" (*CP*, 3). Roethke's dim view of the new order of the self is clearly in the ascendancy:

> I have married my hands to perpetual agitation,
> I run, I run to the whistle of money.
>
> Money money money
> Water water water.

The perpetual agitation inherent in a modern society in its search after money is the doom decided for the lost son, and this condition (a false self) has overtaken the flow of a time-ordered pace of the true self ("The lost have their own pace," *CP,* 91). The isolated stanza equating money and water is the crux of the poem because these seemingly opposite images ironically come together; they fuse—with tragic results, just as those other liquids do for Dylan Thomas in the poem "Twenty-four Years," journeying in the direction of the "elementary town" with his "red veins full of money." It is this kind of ironic identification with two types of self-determinants, the search for money in a capitalist society and the search into memory and the unconscious for identity, that presents the speaker as a tragic figure aware of his destiny and demanding a share in it regardless of the cost, even the loss, to his identity.

Burke has noted this couplet with its odd equation and he offers an interesting insight: "You can take it as a law that, in our culture, at a moment of extreme mental anguish, if the sufferer is accurate there will be an accounting of money, too."[9] Burke, however, is misleading in suggesting that because these two images represent society and nature they are antithetical. There is, of course, an empirical truth to what Burke contends for society and nature outside the poem. But Roethke is describing a subrational condition; his speaker is not out in the world of society at this time, and, as I have suggested, if Roethke is dramatizing a prenatal condition in which the speaker's incipient brain is taking on its hereditary code from the parent, then the two types of self (false and true), represented by the two liquids, are contending. The money-water symbol speaks for an easy substitution, as suggested by the quick rhythms; the search for money is substituted for the search for memory (water) in the speaker's mind. The rhythm of the lines, free from punctuation and equating in number both word and syllable, naturally suggests this ironic exchange.

Malkoff characteristically emphasizes the themes of sexual guilt in these two stanzas, "In terror, the child is seen attempting to commit a masturbatory sin against the scheme of things, the 'time-order'; and with this sin is associated an acceptance of society's materialistic view of reality, still another violation of the natural order."[10] There is merit to his argument, although I think it unnecessarily limits the "hands" symbol to a sexual one that too strongly contradicts the prenatal surroundings of the psychically regressed speaker.

The last two stanzas of "The Gibber" funnel the speaker out of "The Pit" in a kind of Dantesque journey through the flashing dark. The alternating line lengths successfully convey the sweeping action here, and, of course, continue the thematic sense of psychic regression:

> These sweeps of light undo me.
> Look, Look, the ditch is running white!
> I've more veins than a tree!
> Kiss me, ashes, I'm falling through a dark swirl.

Along with these self-observations, the speaker still maintains the interrogatory manner of a child and his irrational world, "Has the worm a shadow?/ What do the clouds say?" And birth here is really a return to somewhere he has been before ("Everything has been twice," *CP*, 72).

In the fourth section, "The Return" (the return of father), together with the fifth and final section, "It was beginning winter," Roethke drops his free associative, paratactical manner for a much more "time-ordered," syntactical pace. The return is to experience, to the actual world, but not to the world of perpetual agitation that, although threatening, is essentially outside the poem. The womb-child in "The Gibber," however, has been conditioned by the self-denying forces of society, and that is why the greenhouse world of these last two sections is a temporary one—an echo really of another condition where the child can hope, "It will come again," if he remains still and waits.

The greenhouse is identified for the first time in "The Return," (marking some progress again) in which the house symbol becomes dominant. The parental symbol, too, is focused; "Father Fear" and "primordial milk" refocus into the "Papa" image in what is by now the most oft-quoted stanza in the poem:

> Scurry of warm over small plants.
> Ordnung! ordnung!
> Papa is coming!

The desire for authority and order is realized in the greenhouse where house and field come together. Self and nonself combine here under ideal conditions, thus opposing the sordid presence of false self in the previous section, and this is the place where Papa had resided before the child lost himself and "fell":

> He watered the roses.
> His thumb had a rainbow.
> The stems said, Thank you.
> Dark came early.
>
> That was before. I fell! I fell!
> The worm has moved away.
> My tears are tired.
>
> (CP, 73)

"Dark came early," as it does in the greenhouse season of winter, but dark is also a metaphor for loss, the early loss of father. And it is through darkness, "The way to the boiler was dark./ Dark all the way," that the child comes back to light and Papa:

> Once I stayed all night.
> The light in the morning came slowly over the white
> Snow.

The return, then, brings Papa back to life and light, and it also brings the child back to the natural world as described in psalmodic tones elsewhere in "Unfold! Unfold!":

> I was privy to oily fungus and the algae
>   of standing waters;
> Honored, on my return, by the ancient
>   fellowship of rotten stems.
> I was pure as a worm on a leaf;
>   I cherished the mold's children.
> Beetles sweetened my breath.
> I slept like an insect.

"The Lost Son" in defining a way out of the self, the way out of a death-directed false self, avoids this kind of regenerative animism for the most part. In these last two sections, for example, it is only the rose, the chrysanthemum, and the weeds that contend for the speaker's attention. In these last sections, too, Roethke returns to the rhythms of the opening section by again using monometric lines to slow down to a stasis the shifting line lengths. This sense of stasis is heightened by more than a double number of occurrences in these two sections of twelve stanzas, as opposed to the number in the first section of twelve stanzas. Significantly, the middle two sections with their more frenetic pace are free of the monometric line. Roethke prepares for the last, monosyllabic line of the poem as well, by interspersing his monometric lines with three monosyllabic lines in these last two sections ("Snow," "Air," "Stayed"—all end-stops).

In the last section describing the beginning of winter, the scene is bleak, indeed, but there is a kind of oxymoronic beauty here brought about by Roethke's skillful handling of verbal rhythms; the imagery envisions something stark and cold, yet the easy rhythms proliferate. There is a plethora of nasals along with the repetition, not only of the opening line, but of such key words as "weeds," "bones," "field," "wind," and "swinging." It is an "in-between time":

> The landscape still partly brown:
> The bones of weeds kept swinging in the wind,
> Above the blue snow.

A time, then, for waiting, or a period of stasis in which the speaker waits for a "lively understandable spirit," which, as yet, he does not understand. Undoubtedly, it will be the spirit of animism that takes him, as it does, for example, in the stanza already quoted from "Unfold! Unfold!" and also in the last sections—one of pure animistic affirmation—of "Praise to the End!" and "Meditations of an Old Woman." In a letter to Kenneth Burke, Roethke is quite explicit about evoking the spirit of animism in his poetry, particularly an animism that is superbly disassociated from the human realm:

> I've just finished a long (97 lines) poem ["Praise to the End!"], the last probably from the dark world .... I've been astonished to find that in the last 24 lines of affirmation there is not one reference to anything human except the line:
>
> I've crawled from the mire, alert as a saint or a dog.
>
> And a saint is hardly human. All the other images are fish, birds, animals, etc. ... Onan's folly. But it's a real piece, Jack: it's got power. But God, I need a larger structure; something dramatic: an old story— something. Most of the myths are a bore, to me. Wish I could talk to you about it.[11]

This letter was written in 1948, and, of course, Roethke was to find a larger structure, attempting "something dramatic" in "Meditations of an Old Woman," but, as in all of these major poems, it is "an old story" that Roethke's oracular poetry echoes so well, the stories of Odysseus, Oedipus, Iphigenia, Medea, Joseph, Job, Jonah, and Jesus.

The image of light predominates in these last stanzas, and as in Wordsworth's *The Prelude* the mind discovers itself to be not alone:

> Light traveled over the wide field;
> Stayed.
> The weeds stopped swinging.
> The mind moved, not alone,
> Through the clear air, in the silence.

Roethke's empty house has become filled with light, and with that light, hope for a livelier spirit, for a vision of Dame Kind, that is, the animistic affirmation of his natural surroundings, excluding the human element altogether.[12] Hope at this time is only appropriate in a poem anchored by the statement, "This is my hard time," but Roethke has successfully made a moral plea, through the child speaker, for the restorative powers of nature to ease the human condition beset by chaos, alienation, and loss. Like Whitman before him, part of this commitment to nature necessitates a metaphoric confrontation with death.[13] But whereas Whitman emerges from this confontation, taking to the open road, Roethke does not emerge quite so successfully as Whitman for the simple reason that his time and place in American history will not allow it. Roethke's difficulty is in his trying to reverse in credible terms the direction of his death-wish, here as elsewhere in these long poems, because of his awareness of the mutually corrosive relationship society and nature have within the realm of the subconscious where his death-wish has directed him. It is the recognition by Roethke of both conditions, societal and natural, that define his search for identity: one in terms of money, the other in terms of memory (symbolized by water). Because this search is incipient, these two opposing conditions are never really separated out definitively enough, as they are in the maturer mind behind "North American Sequence," which is the more conscious poem of the definitive journey out of the self into the possibilities of existence and identity. Here, the fusion demanded by the money/water image necessarily confines the search for identity to the fluid regions of the subconscious, and it is the poet's verbal skill to be able to create that subconscious by means of his shifting, almost schizophrenic, rhythms, to make the house/field symbol the controlling one, a symbol of failure to emerge fully into daylight (for the lost son is characteristically on the edge, "An in-between time"), to take to the field or open road, yet remain in the twilight infusing the greenhouse.

If nature is "beautiful" in "The Lost Son," it is because it is housed and cared for (a societal caring) by a "Papa" figure. Outside the greenhouse and the self the field is "frozen"; the spring thaw will not come until "North American Sequence" (the breaking up of the Tittebawasee River). The fact that "The Lost Son" ends out there, in the field—for that is where the action of the last section is centered—should tell the reader that Roethke knew he could not stay in the greenhouse. There is little movement in this scheme of things, yet by having his speaker "wait" at the end, Roethke has at least established a stasis after so much psychic agitation. And this stasis is a balance that brings into focus, into the light of consciousness (as opposed to daylight) a tragic awareness of life and death. To identify the one without the other would be fatal because either alone is outside the human condition; together they are the necessary source of fear and pity for Roethke's tragic form, and for the lost son's awareness of his small survival.

If Roethke is concerned with the nature of creation in the arts generally and poetry in particular, as he says in his essay on identity, and that implicit with this concern is the nature of God himself, then one might ask just how does a poem like "The Lost Son" fit into the scheme of Roethke's principals? There is no explicit mention of God in "The Lost Son," but there is "Father Fear," whom one can assume as a substitute, since God, house, and father often fuse their meanings in "The Lost Son" sequence in the *Praise to the End!* volume.[14] In effect, God takes on the masculine qualities of a father in "The Lost Son," and the poem itself, as an act of creation, emphasizes the sense of hierarchy and order associated with the greenhouse: "Even the hushed forms, the bent yellowy weeds/ Moved in a slow upsway." And it is only the weeds that are present in the frozen world outside the warmth of the greenhouse, a world as yet inaccessible to the lost son. Because the weeds are out there, however ("The bones of weeds kept swinging in the wind"), the lost son finds himself drawn to that outside world, a world of light following upon the darkness of regression for which he has risked identity and death. Here is an interesting departure from the surrounding poems of "The Lost Son" sequence that are mostly concerned with dramatizations of the child's irrationality and animistic affirmations where the sense of death, for the most part, is absent: "Death was not. I lived in a simple drowse" (*CP*, 66). "The Lost Son" is the only poem in the sequence that dramatizes the need for dying, and it is the only poem that perfects a sense of stasis, that is, a mystical sense of stillness for its own sake. There are some infrequent mentions of death in the surrounding sequence of poems, but they are all in the nature of brief announcements of what "The Lost Son" proposes to do, as the last reference in the sequence conditionally asserts: "So alive I could die!" (*CP*, 99).[15] The animism in the surrounding poems is affirmatively alive and more intense than that in "The Lost Son" (see in particular the last sections of "The Long Alley," "A Field of Light," "The Shape of the Fire," and "Praise to the End!"), and for this reason there is very little or nothing of a quiet sense of stasis, of being on the edge between life and death that the last section of "The Lost Son" conveys so well. This central poem gives Roethke a way out, a "going-forward" in the journey out of the self that defines the Roethkean mode of identity, because "The last time I nearly whispered myself away./ I was far back, farther than anybody else" (*CP*, 89). One could say, then, that the animism from the surrounding sequence of poems is conditioned by the central poem, toned down in effect, and made to bear the burden of death. The poetry in "The Lost Son" carries this idea, not only by assertion ("The cows and briars/ Said to me: Die"), but also through the mood of stasis, especially by means of the slowed down, sometimes monometric, rhythms and the barren field imagery. This conditioned animism is what Roethke develops in the subsequent long poems, and brings to perfection in the last of these long poems, "North American Sequence." It is a kind of trope really, what I have called a regenerative pattern in the poetry, and if it succeeds as a defining characteristic of Roethke's poetry, of the Roethkean mode of identity, it is because this regenerative animism is conditioned by the reality of death and stasis, the beginning expression of which is found for the first time in "The Lost Son."

Emphasizing the shifting nature of the mind in "The Lost Son," ("Tell me:/ Which is the way I take"), Roethke lays much stress on repetition—repetition of images, of moods, of rhythmic forms (everything twice), and it is this repetitive form that supports the tragic element in this and subsequent long poems, for only in repetition is the epic theme manifest, the dance between life and death, joy and sorrow, pity and fear. One could say that the shifting nature of the mind that Roethke's repetitive forms create defines a real or dramatic sense of the edge between the lost son and the found father, between the empty house and the full house (flower filled), and between the false self and the true self. As shall be seen in the next two chapters, the patterns of repetition become more prominent in the poetry; it is as if Roethke were extending the length of his poems to accommodate the repetition, while the poetry itself was becoming more and more a therapy for loss in "The long journey out of the self" (*CP*, 193).

Notes

1. *Natural Supernaturalism: Tradition and Revolution in Romantic Literature* (New York: W. W. Norton & Co., 1971), p. 255. *See also* Abrams's "Structure and Style in the Greater Romantic Lyric," in *Romanticism and Consciousness: Essays in Criticism*, ed. Harold Bloom (New York: W. W. Norton & Co., 1970), p. 201.
2. *Essays on the Poetry*, p. 29.
3. Allan Seager, in his biography, *The Glass House*, p. 22, notes the existence of "the field" beyond the greenhouse owned by Roethke's father, a twenty-two acre field of oats where Roethke played as a child.
4. *See* John Vernon, "Theodore Roethke's *Praise to the End!* Poems," *The Iowa Review* 2 (Fall 1971):60-79.
5. *Roethke: An Introduction to the Poetry*, (New York: Columbia University Press, 1966), p. 77.
6. One notes, of course, Roethke's "Open House" (*CP*, 3), but of particular interest here is another poem about a house, "Sale" (*CP*, 32), which is an interesting forerunner to the "empty house" in "The Flight." The "Sale" sees the demise of a fashionable but decadent family estate:

> The hand-painted wall paper, finer than silk,
> The room that the children had never been in,
> All the rings and the relics encrusted with sin
> —And the taint in a blood that was running too thin.

    In a house with "an attic of horrors, a closet of fears," everything must go—emptied for a new beginning.
7. "The Vegetal Radicalism of Theodore Roethke," *Sewanee Review* 58 (Winter 1950): 89.

8. *Roethke, an Introduction*, p. 87.
9. "Vegetal Radicalism," p. 90.
10. *Roethke, an Introduction*, p. 87.
11. *Letters*, p. 147.
12. I have taken the term, *Dame Kind*, from W. H. Auden, who speaks of four distinct kinds of mystical experience in life: the vision of Dame Kind, the vision of Eros, the vision of Agape, and the vision of God. The vision of Dame Kind seems especially appropriate to some of Roethke's poetry for the reason given in the text; also, Auden stresses another condition that becomes manifest in Roethke's "Meditations of an Old Woman," that is, that the experience or vision be "given" as something that at least partly originates outside the visionary's control). See *Forewords and Afterwords* (New York: Random House, 1973), pp. 58-62, 100. As classic descriptions of this kind of vision, Auden refers to Wordsworth's *The Prelude*, the Immortality Ode, "Tintern Abbey," and "The Ruined Cottage."
13. For a description of Whitman's death-wish, *see*, in particular, "Out of the Cradle Endlessly Rocking."
14. The following examples show this relationship to varying degrees: the greenhouse ("There's no filth on a plateau of cinders./ The smoke's from the glory of God," *CP*, 59); house and field:

> Is it you, cold father? Father,
> For whom the minnows sang?

> A house for wisdom; a field for revelation.
>
> (*CP*, 90)

and self or father ("Who ever said God sang in your fat shape?"). There is, of course, the first quoted verse example in this chapter.
15. The other references are: "The dead crow dries on a pole" (*CP*, 80); "The dead slept in my sleeve" (*CP*, 87); "The dead speak noise" (*CP*, 89); and, "I hear a dead tongue halloo" (*CP*, 90).

2

Distancing the Greenhouse:
"Meditations of an Old Woman"

Other echoes
Inhabit the garden. Shall we follow?
Quick said the bird, find them, find them,
Round the corner. Through the first gate,
Into our first world, shall we follow
The deception of the thrush? Into our first world.

                                        T. S. Eliot

As seen in "The Lost Son," the spirit as something soft
and mobile is in quest of shape, a hunt for identity, for God.
It is this mobility of spirit that is continued as a controlling
theme in "Meditations of an Old Woman," or to borrow a
description from Frederick Hoffman: "in Roethke the soul
must always somehow be activated; it cannot rest merely on
a theological premise."[1] Such a premise implies a com-
munal belief in God, which no longer can be taken for
granted; hence, Roethke's hunt of the spirit is actively in the
present, unfinished, in its search for a shape, a definition of

God. But if the spirit is to be mobile, there are times, nevertheless, when it "hardens," as in the last lines of a related poem, "Old Lady's Winter Words," where the hunt becomes solipsistic and self-defeating:

> I fall, more and more,
> Into my own silences.
> In the cold air,
> The spirit
> Hardens.

(CP, 104)

The tone of this passage is in sharp contrast to the affirmative tone ending "Meditations of an Old Woman" with its reference to a spirit "outside me," and, of course, to the ending of "The Lost Son," as well, with its affirmative reference to, "A lively understandable spirit." But with the greater range afforded by the longer poem (over 500 lines), Roethke devoted some thought to, "Shapes stiffening into metal" (*CP*, 169), as well as to the mobile "natural shapes."

The tentative nature of "The Lost Son," that is, the presentation of the poet's psychic agitation, is extended into "Meditations," but the sphere of action is much larger with more attention given to the "field," in this case a garden, rather than the house or indoors; the time scale, too, is broader, shifting between the speaker's youth and then old age. Like "The Lost Son," the "Meditations" sequence is divided into five parts—five poems—and the "drama" of the old woman's meditations leads up to the question used as a title for the final poem, "What Can I Tell My Bones?" The answers, "I stretch in all directions;/ Sometimes I think I'm several," and, "By midnight I love everything alive" (*CP*, 173), are what the lost son had been waiting for, a mystical vision of Dame Kind, "Unprayed-for,/ And final."

Before returning to the structure of the poem, however, there is the question of a model, a specific model for Roethke's old woman. The poet himself reveals that "the protagonist is modeled, in part, after my own mother, now dead, whose favorite reading was the Bible, Jane Austen, and Dostoyevsky—in other words, a gentle, highly articulate old lady believing in the glories of the world, yet fully conscious of its evils" (*SP*, 58). The phrases, "in part" and "in other words," belie perhaps a more primary source and sensibility—Roethke himself—yet Roethke's desire to reach outside himself can not be denied, and his emphasis on his character's articulation and knowledge (or better, wisdom) brings in another possible model: Seager suggests Roethke had in mind the editor and founder of *Botteghe Oscure*, Princess Marguerite Caetani. "Her personal and financial encouragement were very important to Ted in the years following his first submissions in 1948 . . . she was, in a sense, what Europe meant to him. She epitomized in the style of her life, its history, its taste, and the variations of its culture, yet she was, at the same time, an American whom he could approach without strangeness."[2] Despite Roethke's reference to his character's articulation and knowledge and even going so far as to admit an ostensible parallel to the European refinement displayed by Princess Caetani, it is difficult to uncover these particular qualities in the earthy naturalism of the old woman in the poem. Yet the old woman's social criticism of cities, of those "self-involved" inhabitants, displays a kind of wisdom that one might associate with a well-traveled and worldly woman.

With the greenhouse in the background of this sequence, the reader is also reminded of those "three ancient ladies/ Who creaked on the greenhouse ladders" (*CP*, 44), in the greenhouse poem, "Frau Bauman, Frau Schmidt, and Frau Schwartze." Certainly, these women, who actually worked in the father's greenhouse, must have had some effect on the young Roethke. As "ancient ladies" they might well have had an authoritarian hold over the boy-errant, "Crawling on all fours,/ Alive, in a slippery grave" (*CP*, 39). The old woman in "Meditations," besides being articulate and wise, is also irascible and reproachful in her manner (as an ancient lady might be), and one is obliged, therefore, to view this woman as a parental figure.

In addition to a biographical source for Roethke's female character, one can also acknowledge a literary source because of the Eliotic echoes in the sequence.[3] Roethke may have had Eliot's voice in mind, a voice to react against by using Eliot's manner to his own advantage, to take "this Whitmanesque meditative thing of T. S. E. and use it for other ends, use it as well or better."[4] Roethke goes on to describe his purpose in the "Meditations" sequence: "As for the old lady poems, I wanted to create a character for whom such rhythms are indigenous; that she be a dramatic character, not just me . . . . Eliot in the Quartets is a tired, spiritually tired, old man . . . . Is my old lady tired? . . . She's tough, she's brave, she's aware of life, and she would take a congeries of eels over a hassel of bishops any day." If Roethke intended to give a new dramatic direction to Eliot's meditative manner, and if dramatic detachment was his ultimate object, then he failed in the conventional sense, that of the dramatic monologue deploying a conversational idiom. Roethke never really lets go of his greenhouse voice, the lyrical voice of the self, and so he never lets go of the meditative manner; but it is precisely the greenhouse voice that distinguishes his meditations from Eliot's and gives to them their psychically dramatic, even epic, quality.

Roethke's choice of a female voice is not limited, of course, to the "Meditations" sequence. There are a number of other poems in which Roethke seems to regard the adoption of a female sensibility as a way out of the self (*see*, for example, the last stanza of "Words for the Wind," *CP*, 126). As McMichael has noted, it is the woman who is most easily invoked as a mediator between the self and the other; she is the more bestial, the more intuitive, and hence the repository of her mate's recuperative powers (*see* "The Sensualists," "The Young Girl," "Her Reticence," "Her Longing"). It is these qualities that the old woman dwells upon in the "Fourth Meditation":

> What is it to be a woman?
> To be contained, to be a vessel?
> To prefer a window to a door?
> A pool to a river?
> To become lost in a love,
> Yet remain only half aware of the intransient glory?
> To be a mouth, a meal of meat?
> To gaze at a face with the fixed eyes of a spaniel?

Wallace Stevens had used the female voice as a mask in "Sunday Morning," and it may be that Roethke had this source in mind in attempting to project through the voice of a woman a special kind of sensibility and earthiness.

It is clear from the poetry, however, that Roethke is using a mask for his own voice no matter what source or sources are behind the mask, that with a character who is ostensibly "tough," "brave," and "aware of life," he could give expression to the fears and guilt that attended his own manic-depressive nature. In time Roethke would drop the mask altogether, as in "North American Sequence," after having become more reconciled with himself.[5] With the use of an unmasked voice in "The Lost Son," however, one might ask why Roethke assumed a mask at this intermediate stage only to return to his original voice in the last of these sequences? Why, for example, would he not have used the mask in the early sequence when he was consciously ashamed of his fears and guilts? One answer would be that he simply did not think of using a mask, or if he did, he decided he could write a better poem without one—which he in fact did. Either way, when he came to writing the next sequence, the challenge was there: could he write a Lost Son poem using a mask? Obviously he accepted the challenge, hoping to gain an additional perspective, it seems, by using a female persona to sound out his archetypal themes. There is another answer to consider, which answers, also, why the challenge was never really met, and that is Roethke never did change his voice; it was always unmasked; the female persona in the "Meditations" sequence is simply a myth, it does not exist. Consequently, when one comes to "North American Sequence," the Lost Son voice is heard again, only more confident, more prophetic and wise, and rid of the spurious need for masks or personas. But here in the "Meditations" sequence it is the Lost Son personality immediately detected; the tentative, shifting movements of the searching mind are still there.

The most notable feature about "Meditations of an Old Woman" is its seeming lack of argument and definition of character. The sequence defies and resists any cognitive attempt toward framing a reference or even related references within a space-time continuum. In effect, this is the sequence's achievement, its success, because in doing so it can concentrate on one objective: to dramatize the woman's animistic sensibility. Unlike "The Lost Son," there is little or nothing in the way of progressive form from one poem to the next, from a flight to a return, for example; rather, each poem within the sequence is a variation on the woman's change of mood from despair to joy, the central poem, "Her Becoming," showing the least change or shift in mood, and the first and last poems perhaps showing the most. Even the titles of the poems defy any sense of a developing theme, since two are untitled and the one ending in a question terminates the sequence rather than initiates it, leaving the most promising title, one of affirmation, for the middle of the sequence. All of the poems end with an animistic affirmation of life, and all may be said to represent five ways or modes of vision, specifically a vision of nature or Dame Kind.

What provides a sense of continuity, of texture, to the entire sequence is the repetition of imagery within related but varying contexts. Take, for example, the first section of the opening poem and the last section of the closing poem: there are some obvious repetitions in the use of such images as weeds, wind, field, sun, bird, but then there is the not so obvious, like this earlier reference to the greenhouse (heavily disguised): "Elsewhere, in houses, even pails can be sad"; and the later one: "When I walk past a vat, water joggles,/ I no longer cry for green in the midst of cinders." One could go through all the imagery of the first section of the opening poem, treating them as seed, as it were, and trace their growth or flowering at various places throughout the sequence; for example, the metaphor the woman uses to describe her state, "But the rind, often, hates the life within," reappears at the end of the first poem as "dry pods," and again (twice) in the fourth poem as "a chip or shell" and, "The husk lives on, ardent as a seed."

The imagery repeats itself just as the moods of the old woman repeat themselves, and, as William Heyen has shown, the images do not form a hierarchy but function to support the moods of the old woman, whether despairing or joyful; thus, the contrast in tone between, "A bird sings out in solitariness/ A thin harsh song," and, "the far phoebe singing,/ The long plaintive notes floating down," or, "One

sang, then the other,/ The songs tumbling over and under
the glass," and, "Outside, the same sparrows bicker in the
eaves."

Does all this repetition become overbearing in a sequence
of this length? This is a difficult question to answer since it is
clear that Roethke consciously employed this kind of structure to effect what might be called a fivefold vision of
nature—in effect, to use the repetitive structure of a poem
like Eliot's *Quartets* "and use it for other ends, use it as well or
better." Roethke's animism, faceted as it is, and growing out
of the division between the individual and the society he
lives in, goes well beyond the doctrinaire-aesthetic resolu-
tions Eliot manages at the end of his poem:

> All manner of thing shall be well
> When the tongues of flame are in-folded
> Into the crowned knot of fire
> And the fire and the rose are one.

It is the repetitive structure in Roethke's sequence that *is* the
drama, the therapy even, for his character, for himself, not
unlike the simple and repetitive structures of classical
tragedy, the strophes and antistrophes of the chorus attending the lyrical outcry of the protagonist, or the ritual of
repetition in Homeric literature, the formulaic structures
that recur throughout. If the reader accepts Roethke's
poem for what it is, a fivefold vision, then one may be less
resistant to the repetition and what it hopes to achieve,
which leads to the next feature of the poem: the theme of
dying, stasis, and rebirth.

Here, of course, the "Meditations" sequence continues
the theme of "The Lost Son," and it appears that Roethke
develops the sense of stasis arising out of the last movement
of "The Lost Son" by the idea of slowness; thus, the old

woman's only question in the opening section, "How can I rest in the days of my slowness?", generates a controlling theme that terminates in an answer, or realization, for her in the final section of the last poem: "How slowly all things alter." Developing the related theme of the hunting spirit, or soul, ("a slow thing,/ In the changing body") that can sometimes be, "A pulse beyond nothingness," or an affirmation of nothingness ("The spirit says, you are nothing"), Roethke invokes the spirit as an agency of release and rebirth for the old woman into an animistic union with nature ("My spirit rises with the rising wind;/ I'm thick with leaves and tender as a dove"): "What came to me vaguely is now clear,/ As if released by a spirit."

The presence of the greenhouse in the sequence raises some interesting questions; to begin with, just how "present" is the greenhouse? Is the greenhouse strictly a fiction, an imaginative reference the woman periodically makes throughout the sequence, or is it "there," surrounding her as she meditates her condition? My contention is that the woman is speaking from inside the greenhouse, thus extending in her own way the greenhouse-voice of the lost son from the earlier poem; it defines her desire to leave the greenhouse, as well, to extend herself beyond, to imaginatively grasp a world beyond, which is the field. There are only a few references to the greenhouse, the first in the opening poem that seems to be a recollection because of the indefinite article preceding the noun: "Two song sparrows, one within a greenhouse"; a second indirect reference: "The sun loosening the frost on December windows" ("Outside, the same sparrows bicker in the eaves") that takes the greenhouse out of the realm of the woman's memory or imagination and transfers it into a present setting because of the sparrows image; a third indirect reference also occurring in the second poem:

> My geranium is dying, for all I can do,
> Still leaning toward the last place the sun was.
> I've tried I don't know how many times to replant it.
> But these roses: I can wear them by looking away.

The demonstrative pronoun before roses would seem to substantiate the presence of a surrounding greenhouse, and the imperative mood of a subsequent line of self-address, "Look at the far trees at the end of the garden," would also seem to support the setting, if not of a greenhouse, of at least a place, a room with December windows; and the fourth reference in the last of the poems: "I no longer cry for green in the midst of cinders." Whether the old woman is in the greenhouse or elsewhere by a window or windows may not be important. What is important is that the greenhouse is on her mind, and that she tries to distance it from her mind in the last poem: "In the long fields, I leave my father's eye;/ And shake the secrets from my deepest bones."

Turning to the individual poems making up the sequence, the reader can follow the old woman's, "Journey within a journey," as she calls it in the "First Meditation," and see just what this journey entails: an animism conditioned by death. The extended Homeric similes in the third section, for example, ostensibly describe a physical scene, an indulgence in detail for its own sake, yet actually they are emblematic of the spirit's journey ("The movement is forward, after a few wavers"), emphasizing the spirit's struggle to abandon the physical realm, the crab barely alive ("The tail and smaller legs slipping and sliding slowly backward—"), the salmon, "tired, moving up a shallow stream"—both metaphors for the old woman's physically tired condition, "That anguish of concreteness" (*CP*, 92) that is a physical dying. By means of a close syntactical description, Roethke has brought the reader into sympathy with the woman's decadent state, but as the pond-water tries the crab, "So the spirit tries for another life,/ Another way and place in which to continue;" exhaustion of the flesh signals the spirit's beginning.

In the fourth and last section of "First Meditation," Roethke again focuses on his house/field image in terms of "the lost acres at the edge of smoky cities," bringing the reader to the edge, then, of the large dying cities, that place where one can go either forward or backward:

> I have gone into the waste lonely places
> Behind the eye; the lost acres at the edge of smoky
> cities.
> What's beyond never crumbles like an embankment,
> Explodes like a rose, or thrusts wings over the Carib-
> bean.
> There are no pursuing forms, faces on walls:
> Only the motes of dust in the immaculate hallways,
> The darkness of falling hair, the warnings from lint
> and spiders,
> The vines graying to a fine powder.
> There is no riven tree, or lamb dropped by an eagle.

In these lines recalling the "inexorable sadness" from "Dolor," the city is spiritless and unreal, as it is for Eliot. The waste, too, on the outskirts, what is behind the eye, is the unreality of that which never "crumbles," that for which there are no pursuing forms. In these powerful lines the old woman fixes her attention on Homer and what appears to be an indirect allusion to the *Iliad* (8. 247-52), the pursuing form of the eagle dropping a fawn on Zeus' altar as a good omen for the Achaeans. The riven tree is symbolic of another aspect of pursuing form, Zeus' lightning, and here

Roethke is shaping that form to tragedy, to the violence and destruction that man as artist must continually confront and shape into a unique human passion. What is unreal, the motes of dust, the hallways, the darkness of falling hair, must be made into a reality that, "Explodes like a rose, or thrusts wings over the Caribbean."

In the closing stanza the smoky cities give way to the "smoky ridges" of a mountain scene. The spirit finds the cerulean "high in the elm," in the "far phoebe, singing," and like Whitman's bird in "Out of the Cradle Endlessly Rocking," Roethke has a "single" bird "calling and calling," and of course it is the old woman herself calling, her spirit calling for a pursuing form. As in the ending of "The Lost Son," the spirit, described as, "A flame, intense, visible," is moving "over the field" for this woman, "In such times, lacking a god."

In this first poem (and throughout "Meditations") the dense, syntactical rhythms arising from close discursive description afford a good example of what Kenneth Burke describes as the trope of metonymy.[6] In other words, the poetry secures for the speaker (and for the reader) a sense of expectancy on the abstract level, a sense of anticipation of, or waiting for, spirit, God, belief itself, as if it were for the first time. Roethke structures his rhythms around the base of a three- or four-stress line (similar to sections in Eliot's *Four Quartets*) with a significant number of sweeps into a seven-stress line to underscore the theme of the spirit's movement forward.

In the "First Meditation" a waste-land imagery predominates: the field, the obscure hillside, the bleak wind, lost acres, falling hair, the drunken soldier, dry pods, and the stubble together underscore the old woman's despair, "On love's worst ugly day." In the next poem of the sequence, "I'm Here," the speaker reminisces about the past and her youth and the summer garden becomes the epiphanic scene in her memory:

> I remember walking down a path,
> Down wooden steps toward a weedy garden;
> And my dress caught on a rose-brier.
> When I bent to untangle myself,
> The scent of the half-opened buds came up over me.

Still the opening of this second poem invokes a despairing enough mood, deriving in part from the previous poem. The first section presents a disconsolate woman inside her house: "Is it enough?—/ The sun loosening the frost on December windows." She hears "the same sparrows" outside, but has become "tired of tiny noises," and even children:

> The prattle of the young no longer pleases.
> Behind the child's archness
> Lurks the bad animal.

Here is an interesting departure from the woman's account of the sparrows in the previous poem with their "songs tumbling over and under the glass" of the greenhouse. Is this woman's sudden impatience an admonition to the child Roethke, the lost son ("Behind the child's archness/ Lurks the bad animal")? As a feminine mask for Roethke's subconscious, she becomes a surrogate-voice for Roethke's guilt arising out of his Odyssean probe into the unconscious, the forbidden, or the chthonic feminine, in the earlier "Lost Son" sequence. That this old woman demeans the adolescent three times in the present sequence should lend some significance to an underlying theme of guilt in the "Meditations" sequence, and that Roethke should give expression to this guilt, not directly through his own voice, but dramatically through the perceptive vision of an old woman is to see the comprehensiveness Roethke's poetic method entails.

The woman's bitterness toward "adolescence" modulates into the memory of her own adolescence because she is fearful of her present state: "Dare I shrink to a hag?" Roethke's use of intuitive imagery here forces one to make leaps or jumps in association, a process characterizing the fearful mind. For example, the woman says needles and corners perplex her, and that the worst surprise a corner could have is a witch who sleeps with her horse (although qualified by the characteristically Roethkean terminal abstraction: "Some fates are worse"). Needles and corners with their respective physical dimensions terminating in a point certainly reinforce the idea of shrinking; they also suggest a domestic scene that a woman is more apt to be associated with than not, and, to speculate a bit further, the woman's perplexity suggests that her animal nature, her sense of field rather than house, has simply not been domesticated. The horse image juxtaposed with the witch in the corner might offer some difficulty in interpretation were it not for the reference to the woman's love for horses in her youth in the next section. What is here in the old woman's case is a distortion through time and space of the earlier, youthful condition, dramatized by the witch sleeping with her horse, but then, "Some fates are worse," as perhaps being among the motes of dust in "immaculate hallways."

"I was queen of the vale—", says the old woman, abruptly changing her tone in the second section of "I'm Here." Reliving her youth in her memory, she is the "ward" of her spirit "running through the high grass." The alternating line lengths (for the most part, five with three stresses) offer

little difficulty with their carefree suggestion of the movements of a young animal. But the one indented stanza of the
section carries the theme of admonition, of reproach to the
child:

> So much adolescence is an ill-defined dying,
> An intolerable waiting,
> A longing for another place and time.

In the memory of her youth she too is like the lost son,
"running lightly over spongy ground" (*CP*, 54), but it is the
old woman, in the present, who is reproaching the lost son
of the earlier poem; it is "an ill-defined dying." Surely
Roethke must be telling himself, as well as the reader, that
he means to go forward from the lost son condition of
"waiting" and "longing," and that the old woman's "Meditations" are a dramatization of the poet's development from
"The Lost Son" sequence, just as "The Lost Son" dramatizes
a way out—as pointed out in the preceding chapter—of the
surrounding sequence of poems in *Praise to the End!*.

The third section concentrates on two epiphanic scenes
from her memory; one outdoors with, "The scent of the
half-opened buds" invading her senses ("I thought I was
going to smother"), the other indoors when she is sick ("The
whole place shook whenever I got a chill"), suggesting
perhaps an alliance of madness and vision: "I closed my
eyes, and saw small figures dancing,/ A congress of tree-
shrews and rats." The three indented stanzas of this section
serve to comment on the old woman's epiphanies by taking
up the theme of trying the spirit, just as the natural world
had tried her youthful sensibilities both indoors and out.
The spirit, "A thing we feel at evening, and by doors,/ Or
when we stand at the edge of a thicket," is somehow always
at the edge of things, in some rhythmic union with the body:

> The body, delighting in thresholds,
> Rocks in and out of itself.
> A bird, small as a leaf,
> Sings in the first
> Sunlight.

The last three lines with their decreasing order of stresses present the bird (body) and its song (spirit) as a symbol of that union between the two "delighting in thresholds." This particular image is not as simple or shallow as it might appear at first reading, for what Roethke is after is the suggestion of movement and tension by juxtaposing the small and the large: the bird, "small as a leaf," and the more-than-large, the ubiquitous sunlight. Such a pairing of images is certainly common enough; birds and sunlight can be found everywhere. What is unique about Roethke's arrangement of these images is the orderly decreasing line lengths (3-2-1 in metric feet, the same for stress count) suggestive of song rather than speech, and the use of "first" as the end-word in the penultimate line. The simple meaning of this word not only offers a striking qualification for an endless, numberless phenomenon (for the bird behaves as if it is the first sunlight), but also underscores one of the sequence's major themes: the idea of beginning and what it means for the old woman.

The fourth section consists of two stanzas that qualify the affirmative themes in the previous section. Again in the present, somewhere in the greenhouse under or behind December windows, she answers her question at the beginning of the poem, is it enough? Her geranium is dying on the window sill, an ending of life for which there is nothing she "can do," except for "these roses: I can wear them by looking away." Mindful of past and present, she again censures the adolescent while she draws comfort from a

Wordsworthian theme—the mind's power to recollect the after-image:

> The eyes rejoicing in the act of seeing and the fresh
> after-image
> Without staring like a lout, or a moping adolescent;
> Without commotion.

And the garden scene of her memory enables the old woman to see that it *is* enough, that what she sees, "at the end of the garden./ The flat branch of that hemlock holds the last of the sun," is a different experience in time, but no less valid (because it too is a dynamic condition) than the scent of "the half-opened buds" in her memory.

The fifth section repeats the stanzaic pattern of the fourth section, but with an appropriate degree of diminution. The old woman is no longer tired of tiny noises: "Birds are around. I've all the singing I would." Just as the flat branch of the hemlock held the last of the sun, so can she "hold this valley." There is a death-wish here in the animistic urge to be at one with nature ("I'm not far from a stream"), yet it is not a passive surrender to darkness. This woman does not go gently; she is acutely aware of her preparation ("It's not my first dying"), and the concluding stanza describes her defiance: the winds of darkness must become her as she becomes them:

> If the wind means me,
> I'm here!
> Here.

As Malkoff notes, the next poem, "Her Becoming," marks a high point of the spirit's journey, an arriving at mystical illumination. This may be the case, but what is particularly interesting is the shift in imagery in "Her Becoming," from downward to upward. In the first two poems of the sequence the total metaphorical effort of the imagery describes a downward and leveling out direction (for example, "A tree tilts from its roots,/ Toppling down an embankment," "Then down, as we roll like a boat from a wave crest," "Down from behind the last ranges," "Lunging down a hillside," "The long plaintive notes floating down," "Still leaning toward the last place the sun was," "Down wooden steps toward a weedy garden," "Ward of my spirit,/ Running through high grasses"). In this third poem, however, and after, the imagery defines a leveling and upward direction ("Ran ahead of myself,/ Across a field," "Who knows/ The way out of a rose?" "I was light as a seed/ Drifting with the blossoms," "The shape of a lark rises from a stone," "A gust blowing the leaves suddenly upwards," "My spirit rises with the rising wind," "A light wind rises: I become the wind"). In fact, the woman sums up her life in terms of these opposing directions quite appropriately at the conclusion of this central poem: "By swoops of bird, by leaps of fish, I live." But even this condition can be a constricting one for her in the final poem of the sequence when she wishes to be "released from the dreary dance of opposites" in order to "stretch in all directions."

If "Her Becoming" marks a change in the spirit's direction, it also takes up with increasing attention the ills and chaos of modern life introduced in "First Meditation." "The warnings from lint and spiders" become realized in terms of what Coleridge called in his Dejection ode, "That inanimate cold world allowed/ To the poor loveless ever-anxious crowd," and what Roethke's old woman refers to as, "Mutilated souls in cold morgues of obligations." It is interesting to note that with the woman's continued searching for a fuller condition, there is also a responsibility invoked by

Roethke to pay increasing attention to the emptiness and sordidness of human life that has given impetus to that search.

In the opening section of "Her Becoming," the old woman appears to be at her usual place by the window. Her mind is intense, yet she is "without commotion," having learned "to sit quietly," (according to Eliot's plea in "Ash Wednesday"). The witch and the horse have gone from the corner, for at that time she is, "A mad hen in a far corner of the dark," and her "shape" is a "levity." Her mind dwells on innocence: "A spirit plays before me like a child," and the action described is one of ascendance; her auditory imagination, recalling the tone of "The Lost Son" sequence, reaches for the water of memory: "A voice keeps rising in my early sleep,/ A muffled voice, a low sweet watery noise." The line of questions with their usual childlike rhetoric serve to distance the woman from the rational, reducing her character to an almost primitive existence where identity *is* environment:

> I'm where I always was.
> The lily broods. Who knows
> The way out of a rose?

It is this primitive mental condition that approaches a point of stasis. The spirit may be playful, a shape of levity, rising and falling, yet there is another aspect of stasis when the spirit is everywhere and always, and here the condition may be one of ecstasy, of mystical illumination, but it is a limit, an extreme for Roethke, not a norm or dominant mood. In fact, the old woman takes up this issue in the very next section.

"Is it the sea we wish? The sleep of the changeless?" she asks. "Last night I dreamt of a jauntier principle of order,"

she answers, proposing an alternative. Roethke may have
been thinking once again of Eliot who, it will be remembered, says the sea "has many voices,/ Many gods and many
voices." In that first section of "The Dry Salvages" Eliot tries
to establish a significant and symbolic relationship between
the one and the many. Roethke, too, is attending to this
relationship, but he is putting a little more emphasis on the
notion of many, a "jauntier principle," with which, in effect,
he opposes Eliot.

Like the lost son, she "listened like a beast," and, "All
natural shapes became symbolical." These are the "few"
objects that, in her view, praise the Lord, but in the last five
stanzas she attempts to transcend even the "few" in order to
arrive at some sense of stasis, or perhaps mysticism, even at
the risk of losing the self:

> Did my will die? Did I?
> I said farewell to sighs,
> Once to the toad,
> Once to the frog,
> And once to my flowing thighs.

I can not help but note with interest that these fantasy
flights transcending self immediately follow those other
expressions of selflessness, stillness, or stasis: "The nerve-
less constriction of surfaces—/ Machines, machines, loveless, temporal." The one kind of stasis begets the other, and
in so doing provides some tension to what otherwise Denis
Donoghue has described as too much fantasia, too strained
an effort to be serene, hence a certain slackness in the
poetry. Donoghue notes that the presence of the fourth
poem, "Fourth Meditation," with its social criticism, pre-
vents Roethke from falling into solipsism,[7] and if one takes
a closer look at the structure of the sequence, it will be noted

that the poem is between the more ecstatic poems, "Her Becoming" and "What Can I Tell My Bones?", providing, then, some tension and balance in the same manner as do the second and third sections with their opposing forms of stasis.

If one bears in mind that Roethke's sense of stasis is twofold—the machine and the mystical—then one can partially define that area or realm wherein Roethke exerts his "true" self.[8] It may be that Roethke's voice in the "Meditations" sequence is still pondering or experimenting with the mystical as the way of identity, for the old woman can say (in this same third section):

> Out, out, you secret beasts,
> You birds, you western birds.
> One follows fire. One does.
> My breath is more than yours.

The, "One does," belies a tone of diffidence here, yet this diffidence is a source of ambivalence that characterized Roethke throughout his career. At this point one can note the two paths that will develop for Roethke, the one leading to the "North American Sequence" where he does, in fact, follow "western birds" and adopts, or I should say, develops his sacramental view of nature; the other, of course, is the mystical path, as expressed in "The Abyss" ("Being, not doing, is my first joy") and some of the poems in "Sequence, Sometimes Metaphysical," but there is the qualification, "Sometimes," warning the reader in the title of this sequence that Roethke's aims were comprehensive rather than definitive. In the first poem of that sequence, however, Roethke says, "I live between the heron and the wren,/ Beasts of the hill and serpents of the den" (*CP*, 239); it is this

"between" quality ("The edge is what I have," *CP*, 239) that
I think defines the Roethkean mode and gives to the poetry
its particular lyric appeal, its sense of action and "honest
presence."[9]

In the final section of "Her Becoming" the old woman
appears to "progress" forward from Roethke's lost son condition of waiting, of being "still," by surrendering herself to
a state of motion ("By swoops of bird, by leaps of fish, I
live"). If the lost son proclaimed light as a condition of joy,
then the old woman proclaims a fuller condition, as
Roethke gives her the field (no longer "frozen") and the
wind in addition to the "long light"; and also, of course, the
spirit rises: "A light wind rises: I become the wind."

Each of the last two poems of the "Meditations" sequence
has three rather than four or five sections, and in the last
poem these sections are of nearly equal length, lending then
a balanced tone to the woman's final arguments about existence. In the "Fourth Meditation" the first and third sections dwell mainly on the theme of death. The individuat-
ing sense of death exhibited by the woman counters the
long second section (equal in length to the first and third)
that treats yet another kind of death for her: the death of
society. Roethke has given his persona a prolonged death-
wish expressible in the opposing terms of the individual and
of society.

In questioning her identity as a woman in the first stanza,
the old woman refers to the bestial qualities of human
nature, the irrational with which Roethke has associated the
female. If the irrational or intuitive is valued, it is because it
offers a way out from the "false" self "to become lost in a
love,/ Yet remain only half aware of the intransient glory"),
which is "The adolescent personality for recognition in the
'real' world" (*SP*, 41), or even "the world of men" (*CP*, 136).
It is such "Self-involved" people that the woman speaks of

in the next stanza. Identification is made between self and object or "bulk": "Women who become their possessions,/ Shapes stiffening into metal," yet another kind of stasis, and another death-wish. One comes to death by metal (societal death) as well as death by water (natural death); both are forms of stasis between which Roethke develops his sense of life-giving rhythm.

The third stanza offers a prescription with evangelical zeal; because these "cat-like immaculate creatures/ For whom the world works"[10] are beyond the help of a "roaring boy" (surely a reference to Hart Crane and possibly to Dylan Thomas, *see SP*, 87) and "the sleek captains of intuition" (Roethke himself), there is left only hope: "How I wish them awake!/ May the high flower of the hay climb into their hearts."

Hope leads to a dramatization of redemption for these "self-involved" as "figures walking in a greeny garden," which is the Eden of her trancelike epiphanies as she had recounted them in "I'm Here." The long lines of this fourth stanza dramatize a history of human evolution, and for this reason it should be compared to that other passage about human evolution, the prenatal condition of the child-character central to "The Lost Son." These redeemed figures the old woman speaks of—"The gentle and beautiful still-to-be-born," she calls them—are, "The descendants of the playful tree-shrew that survived the archaic killers." To avoid a seeming contradiction, I take the "still-to-be-born" phrase to mean that these descendants of the tree-shrew are incipient and have yet to descend into the world of generation as we know it; they might be thought of in terms of Blake's mythical identities that pass through different states of existence, such as, Ulro, Generation, or Beulah. What the old woman is doing, of course, is sanctifying the animal over the human, that is, the innocence of animal life as depicted by the small, the soft, the nimble in the mouselike quality of the shrew (as well as her own shrewlike qualities).But who are the "archaic killers"? The remainder of the section is given over to their summary identity: "The fang and the claw, the club and the knout, the irrational edict,/ The fury of the hate-driven zealot, the meanness of the human weasel." These are qualities that characterize Blake's Elect class of men, but whether Roethke had Blake in mind is of no real concern because it is enough to recognize the universal in these traits. It is especially perceptive of Roethke to have his persona single out zeal as a bane to human existence, or at least misdirected zeal that so often has destructive consequences, not only for the zealot, but for his or her associates as well. One might be observing an awareness on the part of Roethke of his own zeal in "establishing a personal identity" amidst the chaos of modern life, a zeal that could degenerate into self-righteous pomposity, shorn of any human and tragic definition. The "human weasel," apart from its colloquial meaning of miserliness, appears to be a composite identity, part archaic killer and part, "The gentle and beautiful still-to-be-born," yet he survives the archaic killers like his mythical counterpart, and this survival is one of evolution: "when at last he grew a thumb." The woman's description of him echoes Roethke's description of the lost son, only here it is not so much a prenatal condition that is being described as it is an evolutionary step toward some mythic birth of, "The gentle and beautiful" for all humanity:

> A prince of small beginnings, enduring the slow
> stretches of change,
> Who spoke first in the coarse short-hand of the sublim-
> inal depths,
> Made from his terror and dismay a grave philosophical
> language.

The far-reaching, optimistic claims of the woman here contrast sharply with the pessimism of the speaker in the corresponding passage of "The Lost Son" where he sounds out humanity's doom and the easy substitution of money for water.

The third and last section of "Fourth Meditation" returns to the woman's death-wish, which complements her death of spirit ("there is no song") in the first section and death by metal (hence death of society) in the second section, for it becomes death by water: "I'm in love with the dead! My whole forehead's a noise!/ On a dark day I walk straight toward the rain." The last stanza, however, picks up the regenerative theme after the line, "My back creaks with the dawn," and then there is some sense of beginning: "Near the graves of the great dead,/ Even the stones speak."

In the last poem, "What Can I Tell My Bones?", the opening section continues what is by that time the predominant theme, the woman's uncertainty about the spirit's journey. As a "Perpetual beginner," the soul is a "Pulse beyond nothingness,/ A fearful ignorance." Her anxiety is all consuming as "shapes make me afraid," and the few "natural objects" mentioned ("The reality of straw," "the sad animals," "wind," "leaves") fail to praise in this instance. The tone of futility and despair is heightened by an intuitive or deep image closing the section:

> A man chasing a cat
> With a broken umbrella,
> Crying softly,

an image of sexual impotence and of a reciprocal relation between body and spirit: the one hunts the other that keeps "the spirit spare" (*CP*, 3). The relationship, then, is perpetually suspended above the constrictions of identity and is reduced, in physical terms, to the merest manifestation of motion (see "The Manifestation," CP, 235). But the old woman fears the spiritual because she fears the body's (shape) consumption by it ("O my bones"); she is in a state of remorse because she still vacillates between extremes that are cut off from each other (life and death) rather than regeneratively related to each other. Here she again offers a striking comparison to the lost son because he is much closer to the spiritual than she; his bones are young, even soft, and not yet calcified into a stiffening shape: "I shook the softening chalk of my bones,/ Saying,/ Snail, snail, glister me forward" (CP, 53), or elsewhere in seeking spirit: "Come to me milk-nose. I need a loan of the quick./ There's no joy in soft bones" (CP, 59). Roethke's man-cat-umbrella image explodes with an implied array of sordid images: from drainpipes to wet feet to the poverty of the umbrella's owner; "crying softly" only adds pathos.

In the second section the woman's despairing mood continues; her opening line refutes the Eliotic condition of complete simplicity when all things are well because, "The spirit" says to her "you are nothing." This mortification of the self leads up to the crucial question in the fifth stanza: "The cause of God in me—has it gone?" The question is devastating because of the possibility of its truth for the woman. This is the ultimate question for her, and it is as agonizingly existential for her as it is for Job when he comes to the same plight (chapter 19). She exhibits the same psychic pattern of behavior as Job when, after seeing her insignificance, she is driven to asserting her own claim of faith and belief in the closing stanzas of the section.

At first her utterances are anguished pleas for deliverance: "Mother, mother of us all, tell me where I am!/ O to be delivered from the rational into the realm of pure song." But Roethke does not end her drama here; had he done so he would be merely giving expression to an infantile wish for release. Rather, she comes to realize the paradox, the tragedy, of her condition, which is to understand it:

> To try to become like God
> Is far from becoming God.
> O, but I seek and care!

The concluding stanza with its Blakean assertion, "God has need of me,"[11] introduces her assertion of belief (and Roethke's as well): "The dead love the unborn." The key word, of course, is "unborn" with its resonance of "The Lost Son" theme, that is, the prenatal condition of the child dramatizing the mythic union of life and death. It is to Roethke's poetic merit that he should link the earlier theme with the old woman's condition, for in her own way she, too, is alone like the child in the womb, "I rock in my own dark," and because death for her is imminent, any notion of God she structures for herself should include the notion of death itself. As the last stanza of the first section introduced the mood of the second, so this last stanza of the second introduces the old woman's mood of affirmation in the final section of the poem.

The weed image opening the third section appears in an altered context from that same image opening the sequence ("The weeds hiss at the edge of the field"), for the "Weeds turn toward the wind weed-skeletons," a complex image suggesting the woman's understanding of death-in-life and life-in-death. With only one question posed, compared to four in the previous section, the affirmative tone takes control as she finds herself granted the "permission" to "love everything alive." Roethke is, of course, giving his character a vision of Dame Kind, that animistic identification with her natural surroundings, excluding the human; thus, a vision, because she has no control over it, that is, no willful control over it:

> What came to me vaguely is now clear
> As if released by a spirit,
> Or agency outside me.
> Unprayed-for,
> And final.

The reason she gives for this vision, "Yea, I have gone and stayed," is not only an acknowledgment of her journey to a state of nothingness ("The spirit says, you are nothing") in the previous section, but also an acknowledgment of the lost son's stay or "wait" in the twilight of the greenhouse, at the edge of the human world. As with the other allusions to the lost son, Roethke here upstages his persona, but it is to his credit to have dramatized the meaning of spirit for his persona in the preceding four poems, that it is a sense of beginning, a return to the first world, and a sense of rising and falling in mood, a vacillation between extremes.[12] In this last poem when the woman's spirit rises ("My spirit rises with the rising wind"), there is a sense of release to an other spirit rather than hers, perhaps the spirit of God that is in need of her as she is in need of it, for it is this other spirit that one encounters at the beginning of the sequence: "The spirit moves, but not always upward," and it is this other spirit that says, as well, she is nothing.

The woman's vision of Dame Kind, then, releases her "from the dreary dance of opposites" (which can be, as well, "the cold fleshless kiss of contraries"), from the greenhouse: "I no longer cry for green in the midst of cinders," and, of course, from father: "In the long fields, I leave my father's eye." It should be clear by now that Roethke uses his persona to distance the greenhouse from himself. By dropping his persona in the next sequence, Roethke leaves his mother's eye to pursue the long fields of "North American Sequence," for here he offers a fuller perspective of himself, his parents, and the greenhouse.

Roethke's use of "final" in the closing stanza has a ring of authority to it that is perhaps too severe for an ending to a poem that is valuable for its dynamism and idea of process. But this finality is outside the character's control; she demands that it be there, or remain there, just as there is a spirit, or a sense of God, outside and apart from the human condition she describes for herself, and it is this distance between self and God, or spirit, that makes possible a tragic form. Complete loss of self and mystical union with the other (God, or spirit, or in this case, Dame Kind) weakens that form, both in life and literature, but at the same time the reality of its rare occurrences justifies the tragic direction that life and, more often, literature so often take.

Despite the fact that repetitive structure is the most compelling feature of the sequence, that the vacillating moods of the old woman might sometimes become oppressive to the reader, that the joyful sense of animism ending each of the poems is itself repetitive, thus giving rise to some degree of diffusion, there is still an impressive amount of ground covered by Roethke: the allusions to "The Lost Son," to Homer, to Eliot, to the sweep of human character from the "moping adolescent" to the "self-involved" and, "The young, brow-beaten into a baleful silence,/ Frozen by a father's lip, a mother's failure to answer," from these and other indictments of society to one of meliorative evolution, "The gentle and beautiful still-to-be-born." In a way the sequence resonates rather than develops; the old woman must vacillate continually between opposites or extremes, between the machine and the mystical, regenerating her identity in the process by acknowledging her dying condition, like her geranium, "Still leaning toward the last place the sun was," but reborn in the consumption: "these roses: I can wear them by looking away."

Notes

1. *Essays on the Poetry*, p. 108.
2. *The Glass House*, p. 179.
3. *Essays on the Poetry*, pp. 183, 184.
4. *Letters*, p. 231.
5. As Stanley Kunitz states in his interview for *Salmagundi*, no. 22-23 (Spring/ Summer 1973): "Nearly all his adult life he [Roethke] was a manic-depressive, subject to intermittent crack-ups of devastating violence. In the beginning he was terribly ashamed of these episodes and tried to conceal them, even from his closest friends. When he was sent away to a mental hospital, he had pretended he had gone off on a vacation. The onset of his best work coincided with his discovery that he need not feel guilty about his illness; that it was a condition he could explore and use; that it was, in fact, convertible into daemonic energy, the driving power of imagination" (p. 79).
6. *A Grammar of Motives* (Berkeley, California: University of California Press, 1969), pp. 505-507.
7. *Essays on the Poetry*, p. 156.
8. To draw a parallel with Blake's system, one could say that Roethke's world of value corresponds to Blake's world of Generation—the actual world—that itself is between a lower world of inanimate stone, Ulro, and an upper world of tensionless bliss, or mystical escape, Beulah (the uncommitted world of Thel). Eden is the ultimate vision for Blake where all forms are identified within the human imagination, a world of "total metaphor," according to Northrop Frye. It is toward this ultimate vision that Roethke's poetry is directed, as shall be seen in "North American Sequence," but in the meantime the mystical and the machine similarly define opposing borders to a natural world of generation,

> A bit of water caught in a wrinkled crevice,
> A pool riding and shining with the river,
> Dipping up and down in the ripples,
> Tilting back the sunlight.

9. Louis Simpson uses this term to describe much of contemporary poetry, a poetry that keeps "its ears open, letting the subject speak for itself"; *Introduction to Poetry*, 2nd ed. (New York: St. Martin's Press, 1972), p. 33.
10. Perhaps a faint allusion to F. Scott Fitzgerald's description of Nicole in *Tender is the Night*.

11. *See* Blake's "There is No Natural Religion" (Second Series).

12. The vacillation this woman displays (and Roethke himself) throughout the sequence, a vacillation between joy and despair, might itself be described as that "dreary dance of opposites" from which she wants to escape into a "still joy" or vision, as at the end of the sequence. Yet the transformation from the one condition to the other is not that simple, that is, one is not forgotten for the other. Here, I think, Yeats's poem, "Vacillation," might be of some help in revealing just what this transformation involves, namely, the regenerative theme of death and rebirth that itself, be it vision, joy, or tragic understanding, makes meaningful the extremes, the opposites, or the two halves, as Yeats describes them:

> A tree there is that from its topmost bough
> Is half all glittering flame and half all green
> Abounding foliage moistened with the dew;
> And half is half and yet is all the scene;
> And half and half consume what they renew,
> And he that Attis' image hangs between
> That staring fury and the blind lush leaf
> May know not what he knows, but knows not grief.

One might say that Roethke's old woman hangs "Attis' image" between her opposite moods, or even her conception of opposites, the "half and half"; that she is aware that they "consume what they renew," and that perhaps this is why she is so apprehensive about the idea of regeneration ("Beware those perpetual beginnings,/ Thinning the soul's substance") in the last poem, "What Can I Tell My Bones?" It is not really until the "North American Sequence" that Roethke drops this apprehension and fully engages his regenerative themes: "Out of these nothings/—All beginnings come" (*CP*, 188).

3

The Shape of Roses: "North American Sequence"

Emptiness is the beginning of all things.
—Ezra Pound ("Canto 54")

The notion of finality that closes the "Meditations of an Old Woman" sequence is somewhat of a pervasive theme in Roethke's poetry, having a particular meaning for him that has helped to structure his edge, his approach to poetry, or as the speaker says in "The Dying Man": I am that final thing,/ A man learning to sing. This paradoxical relationship between beginnings and ends is what Roethke defines for his readers—even in the title, "Praise to the End!" of "The Lost Son" sequence. It is known that he takes his title from Wordsworth's *The Prelude*, and it is also known that it is not the end Wordsworth is after, but the beginnings, the spots of time. The "end" is praised because it allows the poet his subconscious pursuits, his beginnings recollected through the memory and imagination in order to arrive at what Roethke refers to in the case of Louise Bogan's poetry as "the final perspective" (*SP*, 142). It is in the "North American Sequence" that this final perspective is realized through, "The pure serene of memory in one man," and that man "is the end of things, the final man" (*CP*, 201). The "end of things," however, is not vision and complete loss of self, as it sometimes is for the old woman, rather it is a return to the field, the larger greenhouse in nature where the self is no longer in need of the Rilkean animism she speaks of ("I recover my tenderness by long looking," *CP*, 173, or, "To gaze at a face with the fixed eyes of a spaniel," *CP*, 169).

The diffuseness of form that seems to characterize the last poems of "Meditations of an Old Woman"—her place by the windows overlooking the garden gives way entirely to her vacillating moods of joy and despair—disappears when one comes to "North American Sequence," which is structured by an ordering sense of place, the *genius loci*, that prevails throughout. Again, Roethke echoes intimations of Eliot's *Quartets*, and with Eliot's geographic frames of reference structuring the meanings of his poem, there is a similar emphasis on Roethke's part of the importance of place: "this place, where sea and fresh water meet" (*CP*, 202). Sometimes this diffuseness of form arises out of the risk Roethke takes in developing the notions of near and far ("We walk aware of what is far and close," *CP*, 13), or the small and the great ("God bless the roots!—Body and soul are one!/ The small become the great, the great the small," *CP*, 250). Thus, there sometimes is a slackening, a too ready willingness to lose sight of the near or the small for an expansive embrace of the far and the great ("I become the wind," *CP*, 167, or, "I embrace the world," *CP*, 198). But the successes far outnumber the failures or weaknesses, and Roethke is at his best when he creates the shifting rhythms, whether short or long, that keep the near and far, the great and small, in tension.

There is a pattern to the six poems of "North American Sequence"—somewhat akin to that of the earlier sequence with its vacillating mood and fivefold vision. The later pattern is qualified, on the one hand, by a tempering of the change in moods since only alternate poems (one, three, and five) exhibit a shifting mood from despair to joy, and, on the other hand, by a lesser sense of vision, a vision that includes the human element or what might be called the journey's end, the recognition of another human, as the reference to the father in the last poem suggests.[1] Here, too, the machine and the mystical merge regeneratively. This regenerative pattern is reinforced, also, by a richer texture of imagery than heretofore. In general, it is a field imagery that weaves in and out of varying contexts of growth and decay, yet at the same time preserving a balancing sense of separateness and division: "the yellowish prings of grass poke through the blackened ash,/ And the bunched logs peel in the afternoon sunlight" (CP, 196).

As in the opening of "The Lost Son" and the "Meditations" sequence, the first section of the overture poem, "The Longing," marks a bleak, hard time for the self. "The spirit fails to move forward" while "The slag-heaps fume at the edge of the raw cities," scenes of futility and repression: "Saliva dripping from warm microphones,/ Agony of crucifixion on barstools." While the first section depicts a physical and spiritual sterility ("this sensual emptiness"), marking a point of stasis, the second section proposes an opposing, mystical form of stasis, introducing the rose image ("the rose exceeds us all") and, as has been seen in the "Meditations" sequence, a longing for escape and vision: "I'd be beyond: I'd be beyond the moon." The difference here, however, is that vacillation immediately gives way to a

regenerative pattern as this stillness or stasis functions as a
point of departure into the space-time world of experience
and nature: "from these nothings/—All beginnings come"
("Bare as a bud, and naked as a worm"). Thus, in the third
and last stanza this pattern is exemplified in the appearance
of the line, "the imperishable quiet at the heart of form" (an
allusion, no doubt, to Eliot's "heart of light" in "The Waste
Land" and "Burnt Norton"), which is surrounded, almost
smothered, in fact, by a physical world of process, of beginnings: "I would with the fish, the blackening salmon, and
the mad lemmings,/ The children dancing, the flowers
widening." The sense of place is made evident in these last
lines with a reference to the "Dakotas" and, "In the country
of few lakes." Responding to Eliot's plea in "East Coker"
that old men ought to be explorers, Roethke identifies with
the beginnings of America: "I'll be an Indian," but not the
"Ogalala" of the plains, rather, the "Iroquois" of the lakes, a
distinction pointed out by McMichael. The next poem,
"Meditation at Oyster River," begins, then, the water-earth
cycle Hugh Staples speaks of, with water as that poem's
leitmotif ("Water's my will, and my way").

    The first two sections of "Oyster River" place the poet at
the mouth of the river where it meets "the bay," no doubt
Puget Sound. He is perched on a rock, alone, as perhaps an
Indian might have been, viewing the surrounding country
as his habitat. Civilization is absent except for the quiet
presence of a road: "The doe with its sloped shoulders
loping across the highway." It is essentially a peaceful scene,
but Roethke has introduced with subtle effect the silent and
insistent forces of decay and death: "A fish raven turns on
its perch (a dead tree in the rivermouth)." By means of these
two images, the doe on the abandoned highway and the
raven on the dead tree, the societal and the natural are
joined as a source of death. Thus, the dual nature of self is

drawn into the poetry, the societal self like that of the highway with its threatening presence in the wilderness, and the natural self reaching in like "the tide rustling in, sliding between the ridges of stone,/ The tongues of water, creeping in, quietly."

By now the poet has identified with these natural surroundings, an animistic identification portending death: "Death's face rises afresh,/ Among the shy beasts, the deer at the saltlick" ("With these I would be"), and in the third section, "The flesh takes on the pure poise of the spirit" that the stillness of this natural scene has prepared. It is a "first" knowing, a beginning that proceeds from this sense of nothingness, a beginning taking its shape from the poet's memory, "Of the first trembling of a Michigan brook in April." Again, society and nature are brought together in the closing image of the river with its cargo of ice waiting for the spring thaw. In the oft-quoted lines, the Tattebawasee River "in the time between winter and spring" (recalling the in-between time at the close of "The Lost Son" when the light moved across the "frozen" field) symbolizes the poet's spirit moving forward ("welter of tin cans, pails, old bird nests, a child's shoe riding a log,/ As the piled ice breaks away from the battered spiles"). The "no violence" of the first two sections gives way to the memory of the "blast of dynamite,/ The sudden sucking roar as the culvert loosens its debris of branches and sticks," and the forward movement of both river and spirit is underway without fear of consequences. This is no movement toward stillness, whether physical or spiritual, but away from these ends; it is a tragic direction that the poet undertakes for himself, this need to move forward at all costs. The image of the child's shoe together with those of the bird nests and tin cans invokes the ancillary theme of an American wasteland. Last year's trappings of decay and waste again join the natural and the societal, dramatized in the present tense as an unfinished action in the poet's memory. For Roethke—as for Keats, who noted the relationship in his letters—there is a grace to be seen and felt in the realm of danger, notably a tragic grace as the spirit, "Runs with the intrepid shorebirds—/ How graceful the small before danger."

All the while the poet has been sitting on a rock "up on the cliff-side," and his characteristic pose is caught in the line, "I shift on my rock, and I think." The poet remains in this position for the remainder of the sequence, and as shall be seen in the final poem, the phrase, "I think," is repeated enough to establish this poet's primary mode of existence (and at the same time echo Eliot's injunction in "Gerontion").

In the third poem, "Journey to the Interior," water gives way to earth with a return to the country of few lakes, "the wind-bitten buttes, the canyons." At that time the automobile is added to the "highway" as the intrusive image from modern society. "In the long journey out of the self,/ There are many detours," thus a slipping backwards in order to go forward, as in "The Lost Son," and the agency for the sluggish spirit is the car, again joining nature and society to serve Roethke's wasteland motif. Like the previous poem, the same pattern going from relative quiet to dangerous action emerges. The cautious driver of the car is "wary of rubble and falling stones;" a frightened, lost son figure, he detours down a dry, barren landscape where the ravines are "ugly," and the way is at last blocked "by a fallen fir-tree." From this point of stasis a beginning emerges in the poet's memory that becomes fraught with danger: "I remember how it was to drive in gravel,/ Watching for dangerous down-hill places, where the wheels whined beyond eighty—." It is not surprising, therefore, that during the course of this reckless detour of the memory the poet comes "To a scurry of small dogs and a shriek of children," who, in the opening poem, are described as creatures of innocence: "Happiness left to dogs and children." But innocence followed by images of destruction:

> An old bridge below with a buckled iron railing,
>   broken by some idiot plunger;
> Underneath, the sluggish water running between
>   weeds, broken wheels, tires, stones.
> And all flows past—.

Society and nature take part in a sordid swirl, along with the "idiot plunger" (the tragic figure, perhaps Roethke himself), and for the first time in the poem water is introduced to irrigate the parched landscape. But there is no rebirth, no renewal; the water is sluggish, and the poet is "not moving," only the landscape is moving with its "floating hawks, the jackrabbits, the grazing cattle."

In the third and last section the poet summarizes his condition, his present surroundings of stillness and quiet together with his memory-world of motion; there is no schizophrenic vacillation or shifting as the first stanza— picking up the sinuous rhythms from the closing lines of the previous section—so clearly shows. Unlike the old woman's, his earlier self, Roethke's moods are subordinate to the rhythmic exchange between stillness ("The soul at a stillstand") and the surrounding process of beginning, the latter expressed in the longer lines converging toward the center of the stanza. The water image then provides the regenerative theme absent from the previous section as it combines with flower ("I see the flower of all water") and points ahead to the rose image in the final poem of the sequence. What does the poet learn from all this shifting in and out of memory? There is nothing gratuitous about the

process of regeneration that the poet structures for himself;
it involves a conscious choice of imagery and a sustaining
belief that exacts a commitment, as well, to uncertainty and
the surrender of identity:

> As a blind man, lifting a curtain, knows it is morning,
> I know this change:
> On one side of silence there is no smile.

Beginning a new water-earth cycle, "The Long Waters"
anticipates the rhythms and imagery of the final poem,
"The Rose." There is some self-reproach in this fourth
poem, in the opening section, which is an evident characteristic of the Roethkean mode. The poet rejects the "world
of the dog," in short, his animism, while at the same time
acknowledging his "foolishness with God" for desiring,
"The unsinging fields where no lungs breathe,/ Where light
is stone." The interior landscape of the previous poem, "the
peaks, the black ravines, the rolling mists/ Changing with
every twist of wind," symbolizes, it seems, that other side of
silence, and demands, therefore, his "return" to the present, to "where fire has been,/ To the charred edge of the
sea." With an ingenious choice of imagery, Roethke endows
the present with echoes from the past ("Where fresh and
salt waters meet") by calling for a return, as well, to the
charred cinder floors of the greenhouse ("The way to the
boiler . . .," *CP*, 57). In referring to the charred edge of the
sea, I assume Roethke is not employing a fiction but referring to an actual geological condition, that is, the volcanic
activity of a previous age from the nearby mountains that
would have left a charred residue of lava by the sea's edge.
    Place, or the poet's present surroundings, is becoming
important, and it too, like the rose, will become a personal
symbol for the poet. Consider the following lines from the
third section:

And the pine, whole with its roots, sinks into the es-
tuary,
Where it leans, tilted east, a perch for osprey,
And a fisherman dawdles over a wooden bridge,
These waves in the sun remind me of flowers.

Roethke follows these lines with the names of particular
flowers ("Mottled tiger," "heliotrope," "morning glory,"
"burdock"), not mentioning the rose that he will later par-
ticularize in his memory—as he has done with these
flowers—in the final poem. All the images in the above lines
have been treated in the earlier poems of the sequence: the
bird on the dead tree in the water, the bridge, the fisherman, and, of course, water, sun, and flowers. The repetition
of these and other images throughout the sequence form
the leitmotifs observed by Hugh Staples, and their reap-
pearance in whatever context is not gratuitous but necessary, constituting a mode of belief for the poet because of
these images' earned generaic value in the poem. There is
nothing especially innovative about this technique; it is the
mark of a good poem, and one can find its skillful use, not
only here, but also in such diverse poems as Eliot's *Quartets*,
Wordsworth's *The Prelude*, and even *Beowulf*.

At the conclusion of the third section, Roethke speaks of
his place on the rocks over the bay, his coming, ("without
courting silence") "To a landlocked bay, where the salt
water is freshened/ By small streams running down under
fallen fir-trees," an allusion here to the fallen fir tree block-
ing the car (a stiff shape emblematic of the false self) in the
previous poem. Movement is sacred in its journey to the sea,
and the entire section is dynamically structured as it re-
volves around the shortest line, "The lily's piercing white," a
point of stasis from which the longer lines regenerate patterns of beginning.

The poet's memory of stone in the next section, however, shows another side of that stasis as, "A vulnerable place": "Neither white nor red, in the dead middle way,/ Where impulse no longer dictates." As has been seen, Roethke continually creates these forms of stasis as a threat to his identity; they represent the risk that must be incurred for the journey to proceed. This particular expression of stasis here is closer to the mystical than the machine, but both harbor the same meaning; it is to know the vulnerable, the other side of silence, "Where impulse no longer dictates," and it is to know that "sand, broken shells, the wreckage of water" are as viable as "slag-heaps," "singular garbage," and "petroleum" in defining the vulnerability of the journey out of the self.

The final, fifth section is an apostrophe to the long waters beyond the bay, "beyond the farthest bloom of the waves." Roethke seems to have risked undue repetition by adding a fifth section (the only fifth section of all the poems in the sequence), as if to bait himself and the reader to see how far into a sense of stasis and being he could go "without courting silence." The spirit has become: "The friend that runs before me on the windy headlands,/ Neither voice nor vision," which takes one back to the old woman's memory of herself ("And then I ran—/ Ahead of myself," *CP*, 166). It is the sea wind that wakes the poet's desire to "Become another thing," the animistic yearning for death, but as shall be seen in "The Rose," the sea wind can also awaken the poet's identity, which is not to become another thing, but to see the difference between things.

"The Far Field," completing the second water-earth cycle, employs the field imagery of "Journey to the Interior," but with greater emphasis on the imagery of decay. Continuing the death-wish ending "The Long Waters," the opening section sets forth the poet's dream of another journey by car down "The road lined with the snow-laden second growth," a road that changes from "glazed tarface to a rubble of stone/ Ending at last in a hopeless sand-rut," and there is societal death again, death by metal, as the car stalls in a snow drift, and "the headlights darken."

In the next section, "the field's end" becomes another metaphor for death as Roethke's memory focuses on the field beyond the greenhouse ("in the corner missed by the mower"):

> Among the tin cans, tires, rusted pipes, broken
>   machinery,—
> One learned of the eternal;
> And in the shrunken face of a dead rat, eaten
>   by rain and ground beetles
> (I found it lying among the rubble of an old coal bin)
> And the tom-cat, caught near the pheasant run,
> Its entrails strewn over the half-grown flowers,
> Blasted to death by the night watchman.

Again, the regenerative pattern emanating from the shortest line in the stanza directed to stasis as the "eternal" radiates the life process of physical decay, death, and birth ("the everchanging flower-dump," "the half-grown flowers"). These are the beginnings, process unconscious of process, and they merge with the rudiments of growth in the preceding section, the image of "snow-laden second growth," as well as the stone, the sand, and the snow.

Of the many wasteland images linking birth and death in the sequence, the tree image is perhaps one of the more prominent, defining, as it does, a leitmotif of decay and deformity.[2] That Roethke found himself identifying with the Indian as explorer is of particular interest in considering the poet's use of the tree image, for together they offer an interesting analogue to a remark by an aged Indian named Black Elk who witnessed the massacre of the Oglala Sioux at Wounded Knee in South Dakota—Yeats could not have said it better: "A people's dream died there. It was a beautiful dream . . . the nation's hoop is broken and scattered. There is no center any longer, and the sacred tree is dead."[3] There is a sense of guilt in the poem for a broken nation, and Roethke seems to have had a collective sense of guilt in mind in composing "North American Sequence," judging from the poet's remarks—somewhat inflated in their solicitous intent for a foundation grant—about the nature of his project:

> I. A sequence of serious poems beginning with a long dirge which will express through suggestive and highly charged symbolic language the guilts we Americans feel as a people for our mistakes and misdeeds in history and time. I believe, in other words, that it behooves us to be humble before the eye of history.
>
> Obviously such an attempt would, indeed, must bring into play great boldness of imagination, poetic and spiritual wisdom, in order to reveal some of the secrets of our enigmatic, vast, shrill, confused and often childish nation. Obviously this would not be chronological, yet would expose some of the lies of history; our triumphs of rage and cunning; our manias, our despairs; our furtive joys. And it would attempt to expiate some of our collective mistakes.[4]

The second paragraph in particular sounds like a therapeutic description of Sophoclean tragedy. Certainly the epic dimension of the voice in the sequence, the Roethkean voice, serves to expose "our triumphs of rage and cunning; our manias, our despairs; our furtive joys" not only here, but also in the other long poems as well. For the most part the sacred tree is dead for Roethke, too, and it is as if the poet must act out the tragedy of America, from the malaise of its modern cities to the dying landscape. The "furtive joys" are in the beginnings, in the regenerative patterns Roethke creates in the sequence, in the small or diminutives in nature ("How graceful the small before danger!"). Thus, the bird and the rose are the poet's symbols countering the degenerative in nature ("the flicker drumming from his dead tree in the chicken-yard," "this rose, in the grove of sun-parched, wind-warped madronas,/ Among the half-dead trees").

Returning to the second section of "The Far Field," Roethke leaves "time and death" for the alternate musings of his animistic mind, "Thinking," then, "Believing" in reincarnation, not into a human form, but some animal form (bird, snake, or lion). Consequently, in the third section the poet can say "I am renewed by death, thought of my death," and at the same time he can characteristically qualify his longing for unity and the "heart of form" by simply stating: "I have come to a still, but not a deep center," as if to expressly take exception with Eliot's "still point" (the distinction has been pointed out by Louis Martz).[5] For Roethke it is always the in-between quality, the edge that is valuable: "My mind moves in more than one place,/ In a country half-land, half-water."

In the last section is encountered an old man, "In robes of green, in garments of adieu," a reference perhaps to Wallace Stevens, or to Roethke himself, but self as representative of the epic or prophetic voice. There is a note of ambivalence in the choice of green, the color of spring, for a man who is ready to die, but as should be expected, it is the green of beginning and not the grey of ending that "the final man," who is "the end of all things," is really in praise of.

With a profound image almost pulling the entire sequence
into focus, Roethke scores the tragic nature of memory:
"Silence of water above a sunken tree:/ The pure serene of
memory in one man."

The final poem, "The Rose," is composed of sections
approximately equal in length, thus emphasizing a structural equilibrium that is further balanced by the presence of
the only monosyllabic line in the sequence, "Stays." "Meditations of an Old Woman" evinced a similar structure in its
last poem, and "The Lost Son," as well, ended with an
increasing number of single stressed lines (including
"Stayed"). In each case, then, it is apparent that Roethke is
after a "final perspective" comprehending both past and
present in the thinking mind of the poet.

The opening section returns to the poet up on the rocks
overlooking the bay. The time is late afternoon; there is
silence, "The sun a ball of fire coming down over the water,/
The last geese crossing against the reflected afterlight." In
the closing stanza the poet can say "I sway outside of myself," echoing the earlier line, "the hawk sways out into the
wind." In this mood approaching another stasis, Roethke
mixes memory and desire with a striking surrealist image of
a new beginning:

> Was it here I wore a crown of birds for a moment
> While on a far point of the rocks
> The light heightened,
> And below, in a mist out of nowhere,
> The first rain gathered?

While there is silence and no violence in this last poem,
there is little in the way of stasis, or of stagnation, as in the
opening poem. What there is of stasis is left for the rose that,
"Stays in its true place,/ Flowering out of the dark" while,

"Our motion continues" (reversing the equation between stillness and motion in "Journey to the Interior").

Roethke answers his own question from the "Meditations of an Old Woman" sequence, "Who knows/ The way out of a rose?," in the second section when he describes the "growing rose" in explicit terms of place. The rose is struggling "Out of the briary hedge" of its own accord; Roethke merely continues this process by freeing the rose in his mind, a metaphorical transplant, as it were, where the mind-rose scans, "Beyond the clover, the ragged hay,/ Beyond the sea-pine, the oak, the wind-tipped madrona," the poet consciously keeping in tension the near and the far, the small and the great.

The concluding stanza is crucial, I think, to understanding that Roethke's rose is primarily a personal symbol. Having freed "this rose in the sea-wind" from its "true place," where fresh and salt waters meet, to its true place, also, in the mind of the poet (exemplifying Wordsworth's "ennobling interchange" between man and nature), the poet can "think of roses, roses,/ White and red, in the wide six-hundred foot greenhouses" together with his father "standing astride the cement benches." The poet is again this side of stasis, of "silence" where one can "smile," and of course this side of that "stone" which is "neither white nor red." The poet has reconstructed the present by means of the past and, conversely, the past by means of the present through imagery common to both. The rose is common to these two experiences that choice and imagery make possible, and by linking the two through his own identity, the poet sharpens that identity, and at the same time reunites the child and the parent. The feminine side of the parental symbol is subtly introduced in the reference to different kinds of roses, cared for by male and female alike, as the child is lifted by the father "high over the four-foot stems, the Mrs. Russells, and his own elaborate hybrids." There is no resolution or fusion of identities here but, rather, a Blakean distinction between identities from which the poet's own emerges: "What need for heaven, then,/ With that man, and those roses." It would seem that the father's presence here in the memory of the poet operates as a catalyst to self-understanding. Reunion with the parent is a substitute for heaven, but even in the ending of the first poem in the "Meditations" sequence the absence of God can promote some conviction: "In such times, lacking a god,/ I am still happy"—such times as when there is

> The cerulean, high in the elm,
> Thin and insistent as a cicada,
> And the far phoebe, singing,
> The long plaintive notes floating down,
> Drifting through leaves, oak and maple.

These are Roethke's best endings, when particularity rather than diffusion is foremost in the poet's mind. When Roethke ends "The Rose" with the line (speaking about "this rose"), "Mine and the sea-wind's," he is not being diffuse in what might appear to be an attempt to mix his identity with the sea wind's; he is literally saying that the rose is "mine" because it belongs in the greenhouse of "my" memory, and it is the sea wind's because it is in the grove of madronas among the half-dead trees.

One should not overvalue the rose's symbolic worth to the point of passing off its significance as an emblem of mystical ecstasy. The rose need not be a symbol of man's central dilemma if taken as a personal symbol for Roethke, just as the briar rose on the Massachusetts coast is a personal symbol for Eliot. For Roethke, as for Eliot, the rose is associated with the poet's memory of a past event or scene. Perhaps the reader should hold this perspective in mind when he comes across the oft-quoted phrase, "the rose exceeds us all," which, out of context, teases one out of thought. The reader can look to "Meditations of an Old Woman" and "The Lost Son" to see that the rose can work in quite an opposite way as a symbol and drive one in a metonymic direction, back into sense, space, and time:

> A ghost from the soul's house?
> I'm where I always was.
> The lily broods. Who knows
> The way out of a rose?
>
> (*CP*, 165)

The third section of the poem employs the recognizable pattern of the central lines describing stasis ("And gently the light enters the sleeping soul,/ A sound so thin it could not woo a bird") surrounded by lines descriptive of motion and process, here the winter scenes of Michigan and the Dakotas, or scenes "in early summer." When Roethke says, "And the wind tries the shape of a tree," he reminds the reader of his old woman's words, "So the spirit tries for another life" (*CP*, 159)—and if one considers the "wasted tree" (*CP*, 49) leitmotif throughout the sequence, Roethke's verb choice, "tries," is seen to be especially apt in a poem about America.

In the "Meditations" sequence the old woman says: "By swoops of bird, by leaps of fish, I live," and in the penultimate stanza of "The Rose," Roethke "tries" these motions through air and water ("the single one/ With all the air to greet him as he flies" and "the dolphin rising from the darkening waves"). With the rose, "Rooted in stone," earth, air, and water take their respective places with "The ball of fire" in the mind of the poet, shaping the rose for the man.

Malkoff's assessment of the sequence, that it is about beauty, being, and God (corresponding, as Malkoff notes, to Roethke's three principal themes countering the chaos of modern life—the way, the means of establishing a personal identify; the nature of creation, that faculty for producing order in the arts; and the nature of God himself), while not out of sympathy with what appears to be within the province of Roethke's interests, has the unsettling effect of having to impose on the poem preconceived notions of these three concepts, however they may vary in the readers' minds.[6] If the poem is about beauty, being, and God, and Roethke's purpose is to establish beginnings, not endings, it seems, then, that Roethke would have one view his sequence as a new beginning, an approach, that would hope to shape these concepts rather than be shaped by them. Roethke mentions "God" only once in the sequence, compared to seven times in "Meditations of an Old Woman," an indication in itself that the poet had distanced himself considerably from any concept of God, but at the same time evincing an acceptance—without any irritable reaching out, like the old woman—of the divine that is part of man's tragic condition. So far as the concept of being is concerned, it can be fairly said that Roethke immerses himself in a world of process, symbolized quite conventionally by the imagery of the contending elements, earth, air, fire, and water. Beauty, other than verbal, does not seem to be the poet's concern, certainly not any conventional notion of beauty that tends to be exclusive of experience rather than inclusive. And Roethke's fidelity to natural process approaches an inclusiveness that does not tolerate abstractions about beauty. When the poet does court the realm of abstraction, it is more a matter of escape, a respite, which readers have come to look upon as points of stasis in the poetry. The joys of this kind of poetry are "furtive" at best, perhaps something very much like Wordsworth's spots of time, which memory, sacred to the imagination, makes available. W. H. Auden, in his introduction to a first volume of poems *The Green Wall*, by one of Roethke's "sons," James Wright, restates the special case for memory in modern poetry in perhaps the same way as Roethke might have thought:

> Given the circumstances of modern life, the feeling that only the memories are real is to be expected. When a man usually lived in the house where his father and grandfather had lived before him, the past still existed in the present, not just as his memories but objectively about him. Today when men change not only their house but their part of the world every few years, their present circumstances become more and more impersonal, subjective memories more and more important.

Notes

1. By a lesser sense of vision, I mean a less pure sense of the vision of Dame Kind (*see* note 12 in chapter one). Vision here, it might be said, is heavily qualified by conventional modes of perception that perhaps make for better poetry, rooted as it is in the world of experience and tragic understanding. All of Roethke's endings affirming an animistic identification with nature are variations on the vision of Dame Kind, and the ending to the "Meditations" sequence would appear to be the purest statement of this vision; but, it has been seen, whenever Roethke creates a sense of revelation of reality in nature, the animal and vegetal in nature, describing such as a personal experience of the *I*, he is approaching, or trying to approach, this purity of vision. Here in "North American Sequence," the *I* is qualified by the presence of the father in the last poem (as it is in "The Lost Son," but not in the "Meditations" sequence, since Roethke's persona is escaping the father's presence: "I leave my father's eye"), and in the penultimate poem, the last section affirming animistic identification, Roethke switches to the third person ("An old man with his feet before the fire"), which could be Roethke himself, or again the father. It might be argued that the presence of the father brings about another kind of vision, what Auden refers to as the vision of Eros: "Like the Vision of Dame Kind, the Vision of Eros is a revelation of creaturely glory, but whereas in the former it is the glory of a multiplicity of nonhuman creatures which is revealed, in the latter it is the glory of a single human being" (*Forewords and*

Afterwords, p. 63), but this particular vision includes an erotic motive—even though transcended, as in Danté's *La Vita Nuova*—that introduces too many complications when considering a parental figure. On the other hand, there is Auden's fourth kind of vision, the vision of God, which Roethke's father-figure might possibly invoke:

> His spirit moves like the monumental wind
> That gentles on a sunny blue plateau.
> He is the end of things, the final man.

(CP, 201)

This is the supreme vision denied to most people, even Roethke, since one can not consider this poet of nature a divine mystic, and it would be impossible for most people, and certainly myself, to judge on the authenticity of one's mystical vision of God. At best, Roethke's purest vision seems to be that of Dame Kind; all his poetry attests to his approaching this kind of vision. It may be that he was trying to achieve a vision of Eros in much of his love poetry, but even here Roethke seems to have fallen short of his goal, as I hope to show in chapter four.

2. *Roethke, an Introduction*, pp. 189,190. *See also* Hugh Staples's "The Rose in the Sea-Wind: A Reading of Theodore Roethke's 'North American Sequence,'" *American Literature* 36 (May 1964): 195, 196.

3. "Bury the Shame at Wounded Knee" (editorial) Washington *Post*, 18 March 1973, sec. K, p. 6.

4. *Letters*, pp. 224, 225.

5. "Recent Poetry: The Elegiac Mode," *Yale Review* 54 (Winter 1965): 296.

6. *Roethke, an Introduction*, pp. 185, 186.

4

The Roethkean Mode

So memory, that strikes a rhyme out of a box,
Or splits a random smell of flowers through glass—
Is it the whip stripped from the lilac tree
One day in spring my father took to me,
Or is it the Sabbatical, unconscious smile
My mother almost brought me once from church
And once only, as I recall–?

*   –Hart Crane*

In these long poems the journey out of the self for Roethke is undertaken primarily to escape the ego, the "adolescent personality," as he calls it, that the poetry effectively resists. And this resistance oftentimes necessitates the *I* in the poems merging with other identities in nature, emphasizing then an almost mystical sense of animism to which the poet continually aspires. This aspiration is perhaps best expressed in the first poem with its ending of hope, of expectancy ("Wait"), but is best realized, however, in the second poem with its fivefold vision of nature expressed in the endings of the five poems making up the

sequence—the last poem of the sequence clearly bringing
into focus the poet's visionary animism. And this aspiration
is perhaps best qualified, that is, given perspective, in the
last poem, where the poet blends the intensity of vision with
his memory of past events that selectively make up his
personal history—thus an emergence of ego, of identity,
but redefined as a functioning perspective within a linguistic accounting of nature.

The personal history in these poems—which can be said
to effectively limit an ego-destroying animism—derives
mostly from the poet's memory of his parents, and so the
parental theme, in effect, makes the personal archetypal,
because the parents become symbols of the primal parents,
the Adam and Eve that structures much of peoples' unconscious lives. To summarize by an oversimplification: the
need for father is expressed in the first poem, the rejection
of father in the second (with a concomitant appeal to the
mother), and a reunion of poet and parents (particularly
the father) in the third poem.

One can, however, summarize with greater clarity the
important implications to be drawn from this critical assessment of the long poems. There are, for example, some
five distinguishing features that might operate as a
paradigm of the Roethkean mode: (1) the *I* of the poems is
generally the poet himself; (2) the present tense is a controlling grammatical form emphasizing *now*; (3) the jagged,
free-verse line predominates, and assonance and consonance take precedence over rhyme; (4) the basic figurative
device is the deep or intuitive image; and (5) there is an
avoidance of formal ideology. Other features, such as the
archetypal themes and the animism, derive from these
structural devices, as they might be called, in ways to be
discussed shortly. Individually, of course, these devices are
characteristic of many other poets, but in this particular

combination they are unique in defining the Roethkean mode that was itself to become a model for so many contemporary poets.

More particularly, the *I* is almost always the poet as archetypal seer, not as a particular individual or an assumed persona. In "The Lost Son" the *I* appeals to the father ("Papa is coming!"), and in "Meditations," to the mother ("Mother, mother of us all, tell me where I am!"). Together, the poems complete the parental symbol that helps define both personally and archetypally the Roethkean *I*, and with the last of the three poems, "North American Sequence," that *I* reappears at Puget Sound as the mature mind of the poet, in effect a first *true* emergence made possible by the powers of memory that have finally placed into perspective the poet's journey out of the self from Michigan to Washington, from an empty house to the greenhouse of his youth, and finally to the open field, "In a country half-land, half-water." Of particular importance in defining the personal aspects of this struggle toward identity is the notion of guilt dramatized in these poems. That the *I* is aware of desire and possible defeat of that desire is to admit a sense of guilt and to define ultimately a tragic *I* always on the edge of existence, the edge of identity, in a world of process and change. It is the *I*'s repetitive raids into this natural world of process, and symbiotically into the unconscious, that could conceivably release a sense of guilt, for in probing the unconscious the poet is fearful of disturbing the dead that include his real parents, as well as his mythic or primal parents. Thus, the dead father in "The Lost Son" is a figure of fear ("Father Fear"), and the dead mother in the "Meditations" sequence is similarly a figure of fear as she is projected through the irascible voice of the old woman scolding the errant child ("So much of adolescence is an ill-defined dying"). But he knows he must disturb the dead, the reality

of which he believes in, in order to structure his own identity, that he himself must undergo a metamorphic death—
hence the death-wish expressed in all of these long poems in
Roethke's own animistic terms. It is not until the last sequence that the *I* itself acknowledges this sense of guilt as a
"foolishness with God," this guilt-engendering "desire" for
death ("The unsinging fields where no lungs breathe"), and
it is at this stage that the Roethkean *I* can appeal to the
parent for protection, rather than fear that parent:
"Mnetha, Mother of Har, protect me/ From the worm's
advance and retreat, from the butterfly's havoc." As Malkoff points out, Mnetha is from Blake's *Tiriel*, and the name
suggests wisdom based on memory.[1] Here, then, the mythic
parent becomes, not a source of fear as it is in "The Lost
Son," but a source of protection from the transient world of
the present, "The dubious sea-change, the heaving sands,
and my tentacled sea-cousins." The *I*, in effect, is conditioned or defined by a balancing relationship between the
past as preserved in the memory and the present "now"
world of experience. It is this sense of balance, too, that
keeps the Roethkean *I* from completely dissolving into mystical ecstasy, or vision, rendering, then, the mystical or
visionary as a supporting function in the poetry rather than
as a primary goal or concern. One might easily dispute this
last point, for one need only refer to the ending of the old
woman's "Meditations" and her given vision, or to a purely
mystical poem like "The Abyss," as examples of Roethke's
"Mysticism." However, I think I have already shown that
Roethke, like Yeats, uses the occult or the mystical for his
particular purpose as a means of journeying out of the self
into the vale of soulmaking to establish a truer sense of
identity.[2] Turning to the second structural feature, Roethke's use of the present tense, one can further qualify the
poet's mysticism as a means and not an end.

A discernible pattern is evident in all of these long poems since the endings are all in the present tense, despite periodic excursions into the poet's memory—sometimes employing the past tense, sometimes the present. And by endings I mean section endings, poem endings, and the endings to the sequences themselves. With this emphasis on the present, the eternal "now," Roethke is surely emphasizing his sense of innocence and beginning, the *I* always on the edge, always discovering itself as an animistic seeker of the other, much like Shelley listening to his skylark ("I am listening now") or Keats to his nightingale ("Darkling, I listen"). The mystical sense arises from the dissolution of past or future as the mind concentrates on the present by "long looking" (*CP*, 173), preferably "with the fixed eyes of a spaniel" (*CP*, 169). In a poem like "The Abyss" the present tense is controlling from beginning to end, as one might expect. But in a poem like "The Rose"—ending the "North American Sequence"—both past (as memory) and present are modulated to effect a personal sense of identity for the *I* speaker, and of course identifying that speaker with Roethke himself, for the human is conditioned by memory, and to lose touch altogether with this fact of human existence is to weaken the poetry on that account. The purely mystical writer is not the tragic writer, because to embrace a single mode of experience at the expense of another or others is to constrict the consciousness of human existence that the tragic view demands, and as has been seen, Roethke's poetry in these long poems continually generates the tragic theme, enough to subordinate his mystical/romantic leanings.

The third structural device is twofold, line length and sound together, since they mutually support one another in practice. The varying line lengths provide a structural support to the speaker's shifting sensibilities as he shapes his journey out of the self; the first two sections of "The Lost Son" offer a good example of this kind of verbal movement. When Roethke wants to create a stasis, a respite from this kind of agitation, like the last two sections, there emerges a pattern of monosyllabic or single stressed lines that effectively stays the action. This overall pattern extends into the two later sequences, as has been seen, with the longer line predominating and generating, therefore, those Whitmanesque verbal sweeps that derive their energy from Roethke's skillful use of assonance and consonance. Having clearly established his management of conventional forms (rhymed stanzaic patterns) in much of the poetry outside these long poems, Roethke must have engaged the free-verse form of the long poems as a means of effecting a less self-conscious, more self-effacing manner, a form commensurate, certainly, with his search for identity. A curious tension exerts itself between Roethke's free-verse rhythms, their dense, syntactical structures, and the mood or tone of loss and alienation inherent in the meaning of the poetry. What I have in mind are the beginning and the end of "The Lost Son" when the *I* is alone in the graveyard and alone in the winter twilight of the greenhouse; or in the later poems, in the regenerative patterns I have described, their verbal energy (a sinuosity afforded by assonance, alliteration, and consonance) gathering in an almost barren, wasteland imagery. Yet it is this kind of tension between a language rich in sound and almost empty of content that defines the metonymic trope and reinstates a vitally metaphorical language. For example, note the following lines from "The Rose" in which the alliteration and assonance accumulate, piling up as it were, while the meaning of the lines never really suggests anything beyond a sense of loneliness and silence—at least from the reader's point of view. Yet Roethke draws the reader in to a sense of underlying mystery in nature that is close to everyone, despite its impenetrability; there is an urgency here, organic with imagery, especially the concluding image:

> I think of the rock singing, and light making its own
>   silence
> At the edge of the ripening meadow, in early summer,
> The moon lolling in the close elm, a shimmer of silver,
> Or that lonely time before the breaking of morning
> When the slow freight winds along the edge of the
>   ravaged hillside,
> And the wind tries the shape of a tree,
> While the moon lingers,
> And a drop of rain water hangs at the tip of a leaf
> Shifting in the wakening sunlight
> Like the eye of a new-caught fish.

For many contemporary poets, Roethke's metonymic use of the language was an updating of Whitman, but with more of an emphasis on a mystical animism and certainly less on the democratic vistas sought out by the earlier poet. Since Whitman, much American poetry has had to struggle with the formalism and complex ironic modes of poets like E. A. Robinson, Robert Frost, and John Crow Ransom, or the complex intellectual symbolism of Yeats and Eliot, and the impersonal-ironic mode of Auden and Stevens. By the thirties of this century, however, a reaction set in, exemplified by the objective poetry being written by William Carlos Williams, although Williams's poetry of "things," somewhat akin to the Roethkean mode, fell short of Roethke's animism and sense of union or becoming with nature. Like many another poet, Roethke undoubtedly shared his disillusionments with modern society with his fellow poets, and he could show them how he had used Whitman by employing a metonymic use of the language with an animistic sense of purpose to dramatize the varying, sometimes schizophrenic, moods of the alienated poet:

> Be with me, Whitman, maker of catalogues:
> For the world invades me again,
> And once more the tongues begin babbling.
> And the terrible hunger for objects quails me.
>
> (*CP*, 220)

His is an oracular poetry that derives much from the last two structural devices I have mentioned: the use of deep or intuitive imagery and the avoidance of any formal ideology in the poetry. Both these devices allow the poet to establish the unconscious and the preconscious as a legitimate medium of communication for the poetry. The image is intended to probe the unconscious and communicate directly within that medium without the encumbrance of conventional linguistic form and discursive reasoning; thus the poet's unconscious, by means of the imagery, becomes linked or simply becomes the reader's unconscious. It could be said the surrealistic image does the same thing, and it does when the poet's intention is to communicate, but when this intention no longer holds, then the obscurantism that so much of surrealist art is prone to generate becomes all too evident.

What may insure the integrity of communication in this Roethkean use of the deep image is the inherent appeal that any unconscious probing makes to archetypal themes, an appeal to racial and parental themes shorn of ideology, and much of Roethke's imagery does try to sound out these themes by means of leaps and jumps in association. Here, it seems, Roethke had his eye on Eliot in distinguishing himself from the elder poet as the "new Jump-boy" in modern poetry,[3] for surely he means jumps into the unconscious, "the Void," as he refers to it in his comments on "The Lost Son" sequence—a void "for schooling the spirit. It is America" (*SP*, 40).

Consider this image, for example, from "The Lost Son": "I'm cold all over. Rub me in father and mother" with its direct appeal to parental reunion, an image that gains in resonance when the reader later comes upon the conplementary tercet intoning the greenhouse as a place of warmth and order:

> Scurry of warm over small plants.
> Ordnung! Ordnung!
> Papa is coming!

That the speaker identifies with the small plants is a foregone conclusion established by the preceding imagery in the poem. Or take this more subtle example from the same poem: "Snail, snail, glister me forward," which probes the theme of birth, and by means of an unusually apt word choice, "glister," associates the image with the subsequent money/water image through an unconscious appeal to the proverb, "All that *glisters* is not gold," from Shakespeare's *The Merchant of Venice* (2.vii). This proverb, in fact, is extremely relevant to the entire Lost Son sequence and strikes to the very nerve of "The Lost Son" itself—dramatizing, as it does, the complex search for identity in terms of money and memory.

So far I have dealt with only the long poems, contending all the while that they define the locus of the Roethkean mode, and for this reason they constitute Roethke's "major" poems. It should be asked, however, just where this mode begins, or becomes manifest, for certainly there is much of Roethke's poetry that is outside this mode. As *a*typical as it

is, Roethke's first volume, *Open House* (1941) can not be
dismissed in total because in it there is one revealing poem,
"The Premonition," that is embryonic of "The Lost Son"
mode of the later poetry. Louis Martz has singled out this
particular poem for its "cultivation of the inner force of
memory." And Martz goes on to say, "it points to the
greenhouse memories that form the still point of his
deepest imaginative existence."[4] But whereas Martz sees
the fulfillment of this "utter naturalness and simplicity of
the language, the subtle use of terminal assonance . . . in
place of formal rhyme; the shimmer of implication in place
of hard conceit; the evocation of a mystery instead of the
sharp precision of idea," in the posthumously published
"Otto," a poem for the poet's father; it must be emphasized
that the fulfillment of the Roethkean mode, which Martz
undoubtedly understands, lies with the longer sequences,
of which "Otto" is a late addition and successful as a poem
for that reason alone.

   "The Premonition" is unique in the *Open House* volume
for its evocation of what was to be Roethke's true style.
There is, however, one other poem that does approach the
Roethkean mode to a lesser degree: "Mid Country Blow,"
which, despite its formal rhymes, shows the sweeping irregular line lengths, the unmasked *I* speaker. And like
"The Premonition" with its deep image ("that face/ Was lost
in a maze of water") evoking mystery or something archetypally significant, the reader finds here as well, that
same evocation of mystery:

> All night and all day the wind roared in the trees,
> Until I could think there were waves rolling high as my
>   bedroom floor;
> When I stood at the window, an elm bough swept to my
>   knees;
> The blue spruce lashed like a surf at the door.

With the publication of Roethke's second volume, *The Lost Son* (1948), the Roethkean mode was established, not only in the case of the title poem, but also in the three longish sequences following "The Lost Son" that make up section four of the volume. For the most part these longer sequences extend the proverbial manner of "The Lost Son" and the larger, *Praise to the End!* sequence of which they form a part ("What a whelm of proverbs," *CP*, 89):

> Can you name it? I can't name it.
> Let's not hurry. The dead don't hurry.
> Who else breathes here? What does the grave say?
> My gates are all caves.
>
> —(*CP*, 59)

It is this proverbial manner, too, that fosters Roethke's use of the deep image, such as the last line above. But when these deep images are used sparingly, as when Roethke gets away from his proverbial manner and adopts his more characteristic rhythms—the regenerative patterns embodied in his free-verse forms—he again comes into his true form, revealing a verbal agility and sensitivity to form:

> Under, under the sheaves,
> Under the blackened leaves,
> Behind the green viscid trellis,
> In the deep grass at the edge of a field,
> Along the low ground dry only in August,—
>
> Was it dust I was kissing?
> A sigh came far.
> Alone, I kissed the skin of a stone;
> Marrow soft, danced in the sand.
>
> —(*CP*, 62, 63)

Note immediately the unmasked *I*, the use of the present
(by means of the participle: "I was kissing"), the jagged line
lengths and the use of assonance (green-field-deep, kissed-
skin, danced-sand) and consonance (blackened-viscid-
ground, dust-kissed-soft), the deep image ("Alone, I kissed
the skin of a stone"), and, of course, the absence of any
formal ideology. Or one might look at the memorable ending of "The Shape of Fire" that begins with its invocation to
light ("To have the whole air!—/ The light, the full sun")
and ends with the image of the vase and flower, Roethke's
simile for the "edge":

> To know that light falls and fills, often without our
>   knowing,
> As an opaque vase fills to the brim from a quick pour-
>   ing,
> Fills and trembles at the edge yet does not flow over,
> Still holding and feeding the stem of the contained
>   flower.

Look however, at those poems in which the Roethkean
mode is absent, those poems that seem to court the Roethkean theme of identity and the journey from the self but
somehow fall short.

The most prominent group is made up of those poems
written in the Yeatsian manner: "Four for Sir John Davies"
and "The Dying Man." There are others: "Otto," for example, composed for Roethke's father, in which the last stanza
becomes a cry, as Louis Martz has described it, overcoming
the embarrassment "at open exclamation: the cry is the full
recognition of his true center, bursting out of this poem's
Yeatsian mode."[5] It is as if the Yeatsian mode was a necessary prelude to the poet's true voice, not only in "Otto"
(posthumously published in *The Far Field*), but also in the
poetry in general. The "open exclamation" of these poems

is most notably contained by means of a formal style in the manner of Yeats. Roethke tries to capture the strong, end-stopped line within a fixed stanzaic pattern, a modified rhyme-royal stanza dispensing with the fifth line and also with one of the two rhymed couplets that types that particular stanza. This form, or for that matter any overt form to which Roethke capitulates, becomes somewhat overbearing in Roethke's hands, drawing attention to itself with Roethke's energy focused on the verbal rhythms and end-stops rather than on the unfolding of an idea or mood. No doubt, Roethke himself was aware of his limitations, as he suggests here in "Four for Sir John Davies," that it may be "other tunes and other wanton beats" that will come to characterize his verse:

> I take this cadence from a man named Yeats;
> I take it, and I give it back again:
> For other tunes and other wanton beats
> Have tossed my heart and fiddled through my brain.
> Yes, I was dancing mad, and how
> That came to be the bears and Yeats would know.

Here Roethke was writing against the grain, evidently hoping to escape subjectivity by this zealous adoption of a formal manner; as one might say, one extreme begets the other.

Martz writes that after the "intimate self-discoveries of *The Lost Son*" a mask was needed for Roethke's "further development," a means to escape the incoherences of the new poems, and Richard Wilbur seems to agree in his own accounting of Roethke's Yeatsian influence.[6] One should note, however, that Roethke never really gave up his Yeatsian manner, despite the successes he found with his own voice in a poem like "The Rose." What Ralph J. Mills, Jr. describes as the spare, and more formal, character of the lyrics in "Sequence, Sometimes Metaphysical" is, in fact, the Yeatsian quality I am speaking of; but whereas Mills sees these lyrics as exemplifying a further stage of visionary experience—an internal rather than an external focus on reality—these Yeatsian lyrics, as they might be called, seem to merely repeat rather than extend the themes discussed heretofore in the long poems. There are poems such as "In a Dark Time," with its concluding stanza echoing Yeats's "The Circus Animals' Desertion" and "Among School Children":

> Dark, dark my light, and darker my desire.
> My soul, like some heat-maddened summer fly,
> Keeps buzzing at the sill. Which I is *I*?
> A fallen man, I climb out of my fear.
> The mind enters itself, and God the mind,
> And one is One, free in the tearing wind,

or "The Sequel," "The Motion," "Infirmity," "The Marrow," "The Tree, the Bird," "The Restored," "The Right Thing," and "Once More, The Round"—all poems repeating the body-spirit theme of the long poems, and echoing, too, Yeats's "A Dialogue of Self and Soul." Consider the following lines from "The Tree, the Bird":

> I was a finger pointing at the moon,
> At ease with joy, a self enchanted man.
> Yet when I sighed, I stood outside my life,
> A leaf unaltered by the midnight scene.

that echo the poet swaying outside himself in "The Rose"; or the closing lines, "Thus I endure this last pure stretch of joy,/ The dire dimensional of a final thing," again echoes "the final man" who is "the end of things" in "The Far Field." And yet again in these lines from "Infirmity,"

Roethke's themes are reiterated from "Meditations of an Old Woman":

> When opposites come suddenly in place,
> I teach my eyes to hear, my ears to see
> How body from spirit slowly does unwind
> Until we are pure spirit at the end.

Yet what is missing in all of these formal lyrics, and precisely what is integral to the long poems, is the vitality of tone so important to the Roethkean voice; one might say the self-conflict that Roethke's free-verse form allows to develop, the formal lyrics do not. Again, consider the poem, "Frau Bauman, Frau Schmidt, and Frau Schwartze," a poem published in 1952 when Roethke's Yeatsian influence was perhaps strongest, so Martz reports. Despite this poem's literary allusion to Yeats's poem, "The Magi" (suggested by Martz), the poem clearly shows the Roethkean mode of the long poems, and like those longer poems, it is the right mixture, a blending, that is, of past and present that gives force to the dramatic *I* in the journey out of the self:

> I remember how they picked me up, a spindly kid,
> Pinching and poking my thin ribs
> Till I lay in their laps, laughing,
> Weak as a whiffet;
> Now, when I'm alone and cold in my bed,
> They still hover over me,
> These ancient leathery crones,
> With their bandannas stiffened with sweat,
> And their thorn-bitten wrists,
> And their snuff-laden breath blowing lightly over me
>   in my first sleep.

There is no dialogue here between body and soul, no romantic ironies, "Which I is *I*?", no paradoxes, "I teach my eyes to hear, my ears to see," but rather the personal drama of an unfolding stage of life—in short, a journey. One might even say that Roethke has utilized the true free-verse form, that it is most convincing when it is giving expression to the journey out of the self. It is only in the last line that the poem even attempts to assert the suggestion of an idea, and it is by means of an image, a deep image, that such is done: " . . . blowing lightly over me in my first sleep."

In "The Dying Man" (dedicated to Yeats: "In Memoriam: W. B. Yeats"), Roethke gives a five-part poem with obvious allusions to Yeats's form and thought, even though the imagery is Roethkean—most of it having appeared in a good many previous poems, as Malkoff has shown.[7] Yet, it is because there are both voices vying, as it were, that again the somewhat imposing sanction of an established metrical form conflicts with, more than enhances, the Roethkean themes of identity, death, and rebirth—themes that are rooted in the tangled inconsistencies of the human condition itself—that "The Dying Man" is not, as Malkoff would have it, "one of Roethke's most personal achievements," but rather a good, carefully constructed poem that misses the perfection of the long poems where the free-verse patterns more readily accommodate the lyrical *I* regeneratively faring forward from the self. For comparison's sake, one could pair off a number of passages to show these structural differences; consider, for example, the following stanza from "The Dying Man" that uses a lost son theme:

> A ghost comes out of the unconscious mind
> To grope my sill: it moans to be reborn!
> The figure at my back is not my friend;
> The hand upon my shoulder turns to horn.
> I found my father when I did my work,
> Only to lose myself in this small dark.

This particular stanza opens the third section entitled, "The Wall," which roughly corresponds to the third section, "The Gibber," in "The Lost Son," insofar as both sections present a kind of impediment or obstacle to the unfolding dramatic action of the larger poem in which each appears. The structural contrast is most enlightening, I think, in revealing the superiority of Roethke's free-verse form in the earlier poem.

The above stanza is the first of three making up "The Wall" section, and it states more than dramatizes the argument of the section. The second stanza continues the argument with a rhetorical question, "What sensual eye can keep an image pure,/ Leaning across a sill to greet the dawn?" Finally, in the third and last stanza a resolution of sorts is attempted by means of a Blakean surrender of identity to other:

> The Wall has entered: I must love the wall,
> A madman staring at perpetual night,
> A spirit raging at the visible.

With a characteristic use of oxymoronic imagery, Roethke ends the section on the road of excess—hoping it leads to the palace of wisdom:

> I breathe alone until my dark is bright.
> Dawn's where the white is. Who would know the dawn
> When there's a dazzling dark behind the sun?

Turing to the third section of "The Lost Son," note a similar argument: the questioning of spirit before the sensuous world of body:

What gliding shape
Beckoning through halls,
stood poised on the stair,
Fell dreamily down?

From the mouths of jugs
Perched on many shelves,
I saw substance flowing
That cold morning.

Like a slither of eels
That watery cheek
As my own tongue kissed
My lips awake.

The section ends, as does its counterpart, with the idea of release, of surrender, again using an oxymoronic imagery:

These sweeps of light undo me.
Look, look, the ditch is running white!
I've more veins than a tree!
Kiss me ashes, I'm falling through a dark swirl.

But how much more vital and urgent is the tone! This urgency is immediately introduced at the beginning of the section:

At the wood's mouth,
By the cave's door,
I listened to something
I had heard before.

And the entire section promotes a real sense of release as the speaker continually sounds the archetypal theme of first parents, "I want the old rage, the lash of primordial milk!", and, "Rub me in father and mother." Roethke's cry for the ultimate reunion of parent and child, however, courts disaster as well: "All the windows are burning! What's left of my life?" ("My veins are running nowhere"), and it is only because this threat of complete dissolution is imminent that the release from this anguished cry for reunion is credible—a release that brings about the memorable "return" to Papa in the next section. In the Yeatsian poem, of course, the mention of father calls into play both real father (papa) and spiritual or literary father, Yeats. The dual role of father here is, however, more dangerously ambivalent than the duality of real father and archetypal father (Adam) in "The Lost Son," simply for the reason that the Yeatsian identity is too precise, forcing not only a prescribed literary form on Roethke's poetic expression, but also conflicting too sharply with the identity of Roethke's real father and thus invoking an unwanted sense of competition between the two.

Moving to one more example in the fifth and last section of "The Dying Man" entitled, "They Sing, They Sing," there is found again the tone that is one of assertion and statement:

> Who thought love but a motion in the mind?
> Am I but nothing, leaning towards a thing?
> I'll scare myself with sighing, or I'll sing;
> Descend, O gentlest light, descend, descend.
> O sweet field far ahead, I hear your birds,
> They sing, they sing, but still in minor thirds.

Looking over to "Meditations of an Old Woman" (which follows "The Dying Man" as the fifth and final section of *Words for the Wind*) at a complementary passage using similar imagery, the free-verse form is more suitable for the action of birds singing, the invoking of the perennial field image, the movement from some higher action (as birds far off) literally down to the immediate sense of the *I*'s presence, the true identity; at the risk of overquotation, I quote the notable last stanza of "First Meditation":

> There are still times morning and evening:
> The cerulean, high in the elm,
> Thin and insistent as a cicada,
> And the far phoebe, singing,
> The long plaintive notes floating down,
> Drifting through leaves, oak and maple,
> Or the whippoorwill, along the smoky ridges,
> A single bird calling and calling;
> A fume reminds me, drifting across wet gravel;
> A cold wind comes over wet stones;
> A flame, intense, visible,
> Plays over the dry pods,
> Runs fitfully along the stubble,
> Moves over the field,
> Without burning.
>   In such times, lacking a god,
>   I am still happy.

What the free-verse form promotes that the established metrical form does not is simply the *I*'s desire for what might be called an innocent scansion of nature, a scansion that catalogues, takes inventory or stock of nature's store without the interference of abstract classifications (like "They sing, they sing, but still in minor thirds"). This Whitmanesque view of nature goes back to Homer, and it would not be wrong to suppose that the Classical temperament behind this mode is one of measurement, not classification, like the neoclassical temperament of the eighteenth and nineteenth centuries.[8] Given Roethke's self-imposed problem of identity and his Anglo-American literary heritage, it is not surprising that he would vacillate between Yeats and Whitman in an effort to create his own voice.

Each of the poems, "The Dying Man" and "Four for Sir John Davies," attempt to convey the theme of sensual love and what it entails for the value-seeking lover, as these lines from the latter poem suggest:

> What shape leaped forward at the sensual cry?—
> Sea-beast or bird flung toward the ravaged shore?
> Did space shake off an angel with a sigh?
> We rose to meet the moon, and saw no more.
> It was and was not she, a shape alone,
> Impaled on light, and whirling slowly down.

Roethke takes up this theme, however, with prolonged attention in the love poems, one group arranged for the *Words for the Wind* (1958) volume, and the other group for *The Far Field* (1964). A careful reading of these poems shows just how the Roethkean mode fares.

As has been seen in the case of the long poems, the poet's journey from the self does not involve the woman as other, unless one accepts without equivocation the female *I* in "Meditations of an Old Woman" as an identity apart from the poet's, an assumption made at considerable risk. Here in the love poems, however, the woman is invoked as a means for the poet to escape himself and become something else, or other. Consequently, there is considerable strain placed on many of these short lyrics to do the work of a visionary poem, a poem of sustained effort, such as the "Meditations" sequence or "The Abyss," that can perhaps better bring the visionary theme to focus. What these poems do best is to present the problem of identity for the speaker, but they do not dramatize it, and for this reason they are merely a prelude to the themes of the long poems.

The first group of sixteen love poems exemplify·Roeth-
ke's metaphysical, formal style, and perhaps the most interesting one from this point of view is "Love's Progress"
that makes an *a*typical reference to the field and to father.
The first three stanzas of this poem posit the possibilities of
the love relationship between the poet and the woman
("The long veins of the vine/ Journey around a tree"). As
usual with the woman in all of these poems, she is closer to
the animal than the poet, and is therefore the link between
the two ("True, she can think a bird/ Until it broods in her
eyes"). In the fourth stanza, then, the leap is made, as it
were, into the animal world of other, but the risk is, or
proves to be, too great, and the sense of loss and attendant
fear completely take over, obscuring whatever "edge"
Roethke might have established:

> It's midnight on the mouse,
> The rabbit, and the wren;
> A log sings in its flame.
> Father, I'm far from home,
> And I have gone nowhere.
>
> The close dark hugs me hard,
> And all the birds are stone.
> I fear for my own joy;
> I fear myself in the field,
> For I would drown in fire.

It is interesting to note here how Roethke may have been
telling himself that the love poetry he was writing could not
fulfill the requirements his quest for identity demanded.
Here Roethke sees his animate, natural world—the natural
shapes—become hardened: "And all the birds are stone";
the same as with the last poem of this group of love poems,
"Memory," where the poet begins in union with the woman,

and ends in separation; there is no sublimation from body to soul like Donne's "The Ecstasy," and hence no successful reaching out to other and establishing an "edge":

> She turns, as if to go,
> Half bird, half animal.
> The wind dies on the hill.
> Love's all. Love's all I know.
>
> A doe drinks by a stream,
> A doe and its fawn.
> When I follow after them,
> The grass changes to stone.

The line, "Love's all. Love's all I know," presents the reader with rather a tame excuse, somewhat irresponsible on the poet's part, as if he were shrugging his shoulders to the problem that one knows he is genuinely concerned with. All these poems take up this problem, and together they define the poet's vacillation—as the "Meditations" sequence does—between despair and joy. Generally, it is the first half of the group that for the most part is much more joyful than the latter half. But unlike the "Meditations" sequence, or the other long poems for that matter, these particular poems are simply not engaging enough to do justice to Roethke's epic themes of selfhood and identity. Of course, the problem is baldly stated in the last stanza of "The Voice":

> Desire exults the ear:
> Bird, girl, and ghostly tree,
> The earth, the solid air—
> Their slow song sang in me;
> The long noon pulsed away,
> Like any summer day,

or in another poem appropriately entitled, "The Other":

> What is she while I live?—
> Who plagues me with her Shape,
> Lifting a nether Lip
> Lightly: so buds unleave;
> But if I move too close,
> Who busks me on the Nose?

If, however, one is to consider the poet's problem of identity, and by implication one's own, one is, nevertheless, obligated by the nature of the poetry itself to consider the identity of the poet's partner, the woman. Now this is a particularly sensitive issue because the reader must ask himself at the outset whether he would have some idealized figure presented to him, or does he wish, in fact, a psychologically engaging figure that the poet is seriously attempting to understand. If Roethke is celebrating sexual love, as he does in "I Knew a Woman" and "Words for the Wind," then perhaps an idealized partner (one who responds without question to the poet's needs) will suffice for that kind of poetry; and conversely, that poetry that despairs of sexual love, as in "The Sensualists":

> "My shoulder bitten from your teeth;
> What's that peculiar smell?
> No matter which one is beneath,
> Each is an animal,"—

the female figure might equally be dismissed without psychological understanding. Inevitably it is the poet's identity that is the problem deserving of importance, and inevitably it is the woman who is undeserving of importance, a mere sounding board that sometimes "squeaks in pure Plato":

The pure admire the pure, and live alone;
I love a woman with an empty face.
Parmenides put Nothingness in place;
She tries to think, and it flies loose again.
How slow the changes of a golden mean:
Great Boehme rooted all in Yes and No;
At times my darling squeaks in pure Plato.
                                                            —(*CP*, 133)

But if the reader demands the "edge" between self and other, as Roethke so skillfully teaches in the long poems, then these love poems fall short of providing that "edge." Woman as other is not developed enough by the poet to give a sense of definition between the poet and the woman, hence not a sense of the "edge" between the two; certainly not the "edge" Roethke shapes in the greenhouse, or at Puget Sound when the other is outside the human realm—where other is nature and, "Where the salmon ease their way into the kelp beds,/ And the sea rearranges itself among the small islands" (*CP*, 205).

In the second group of love poems, consisting of thirteen poems, it is apparent that Roethke wants to objectify his female figure by identifying her in certain poems as his wife, Beatrice (identified expressly in "The Happy Three," "The Shy Man," "Her Wrath," and "Wish for a Young Wife," and impliedly in the remaining poems of the group), and to this extent these poems are an improvement over the first group. No doubt Roethke's late marriage to Beatrice O'Connell (1953), after which these poems were written, provided the needed focus for a more personal love lyric in which the feminine point of view could be given some development. One way in which Roethke implemented this approach was to assume the female voice as he had previously done in the "Meditations of an Old Woman" sequence. Thus, the opening six poems are expressly in the feminine voice, and the last half of the group, the reader then finds, counters back with the masculine voice. I do not want to pass judgment here as to which voice is the most genuinely feminine or masculine (a difficult, perhaps impossible, task), but the fact remains that Roethke is making the effort, despite himself, to extend himself, his lyrical voice to something other, and in so doing he at least captures some of the otherness, a "girlness" really ("And my dress caught on a rose-brier," *CP*, 162), that he manages in parts of the "Meditations" sequence—for example, in the opening poem, "The Young Girl":

> Today I skipped on the shore,
> My eyes neither here nor there,
> My thin arms to and fro,
> A bird my body,
> My bird blood ready.

Another way Roethke objectifies his female figure is to simply stand back and describe her moods in his own voice:

> Inside, my darling wife
> Sharpened a butcher knife;
> Sighed out her pure relief
>   That I was gone.
>
> When I had tried to clean
> My papers up, between
> Words skirting the obscene—
>   She frowned her frown.
>
> —(*CP*, 213)

Despite the chopped-up prose fitted to hold the rhyme, this particular poem, "The Happy Three," presents the trinitarian sense of identity that Roethke is working with in all of these love poems, including the first group, for here is woman, animal ("our goose, Marianne"), and poet brought together at the end of the poem ("Three in the sun"), as if to suggest that only by means of the presence of the animal world can humans live harmoniously together.

The best poems of this second group, however, are those two that complement the Roethkean mode as has been derived and defined from the long poems, and here, as might be expected, the *I* (female voice) takes on its animistic strains, scanning the natural world of other, always becoming. The title of the first poem of the "North American Sequence," "The Longing," becomes engendered into "Her Longing":

> But now—
> The wild stream, the sea itself cannot contain me:
> I dive with the black hag, the cormorant,
> Or walk the pebbly shore with the humpbacked heron,
> Shaking out my catch in the morning sunlight,
> Or rise with the gar-eagle, the great winged condor.
> Floating over the mountains,
> Pitting my breast against the rushing air,
> A phoenix sure of my body,
> Perpetually rising out of myself,
> My wings hovering over the shore birds,
> Or beating against the black clouds of the storm,
> Protecting the sea-cliffs.

And in the other poem, "Her Time," ending by what has come to be expected as Roethke's characteristic abode (like the ending quoted above), the shore line where fresh and sea water meet, the *I* is seen to abandon even the world of men and animals in a timely, and therefore successful, surrender of identity—but only after an "edge" has been established:

> ... before
> The long surf of the storm booms
> Down on the near shore,
> When everything—birds, men, dogs—
> Runs to cover:
> I'm one to follow
> To follow.

In the Yeatsian poems and the love poems as a whole, Roethke falls short of his true mode of expression momentarily realized in "Frau Bauman, Frau Schmidt, and Frau Schwartze" from the former group, and "Her Longing" and "Her Time" from the latter. While the parental theme is perhaps strongest in the Yeatsian poems, it is weakest in the love poems, dealing as they do with the adult or mature *I*. But in the long poem ("the long greenhouse") it is inevitable that the poet return to his self-defining parental theme:

> Dark all the way,
> Over slippery cinders
> Through the long greenhouse.

Notes

1. *Roethke, an Introduction*, p. 182.
2. In the famous letter to George and Georgiana Keats (21 April 1819), it will be remembered, Keats speaks about the soulmaking ability in man as that of acquiring a personal identity for his impersonal God-given intelligence, and this process (going from the impersonal to the personal, showing, therefore, that existence is possible) requires the individual to engage experience, getting on with life, as it were: "Do you not see how necessary a World of Pains and troubles is to school an Intelligence and make it a soul?" or in modern

terms, to paraphrase Roethke, a place such as the void, the unconscious, for schooling the spirit.

3. "Everybody is tired of Tiresome Tom, the Cautious Cardinal, and wants to hear about the new jump-boy, the master of diddle-we-care-couldly" (letter to Kenneth Burke, *Letters*, p. 154). The distinction here is not all that neat, as Roethke admits in another letter to Ralph Mills, Jr.: "it is one thing to make amazing metaphors as opposites on a string—this Thomas does, but rarely does he go in for real *jumps* in association . . . . Eliot does, bastard that he is, and so does Crane; but Crane's sense for language sometimes betrays him and also his sense for a total unity" (p. 251).

4. *Essays on the Poetry*, p. 21.

5. *Essays on the Poetry*, p. 22.

6. "Poetry's Debt to Poetry," pp. 278-80.

7. *Roethke, an Introduction*, p. 151.

8. Alfred North Whitehead's *Science and the Modern World* (New York: Macmillan, 1925) sheds much light on this issue: "The practical counsel to be derived from Pythagoras, is to measure, and thus to express quality in terms of numerically determined quantity. But the biological sciences, then and till our own time, have been overwhelmingly classificatory . . . . Classification is a halfway house between the immediate concreteness of the individual thing and the complete abstraction of mathematical notions" (p. 41).

5

The Legacy of Roethke

The fire which Prometheus stole was the means by which man demanded a new destiny, and took on the guilt of achieving it. Fire enabled them to move from nature to culture, but it made culture a dangerous possession: it made tragedy probable.

Denis Donoghue

The deep image, so important to Roethke's poetry, appears to have been a term coined by Jerome Rothenberg, who along with Robert Kelly, Robert Bly, and Robert Creeley, recognized a different kind of imagistic poetry—from that defined by Pound—in the poetry of France, Germany, Spain, and Latin America, a surrealistic poetry that imagistically communicates through the unconscious.[1] Today, of course, readers have become accustomed to this kind of poetry, but little or no credit has been given to Roethke for initiating in this country, largely on his own, a poetry of the deep image, especially its innovative beginnings in "The Lost Son" sequence. That such poetry is meant to be therapeutic is self-evident; for Roethke the therapy lies in "schooling the spirit," a way of transcending (or is it combating?) the encrustations of a technocratic, consumer society. For other poets with similar feelings, the Roethkean mode was already there as a striking American model—an urgent, oracular poetry, probing the unconscious by means of the lyrical *I* engaging the deep image that their mentor had patterned for them in his long poems. Pursuing these ends, poets writing in America were fulfilling de Tocqueville's "remarkable prophecy," as Auden termed it, that such poets living in a democracy becoming increasingly incomprehensible to them would turn in on themselves, "read their inner soul" for the values they searched after.[2]

The following five poets exemplify not only this inward direction, but also, and more important, the Roethkean manner in which they take it, for better or worse. Each of these poets acknowledged Roethke outside their poetry, but more important, it is their poetry that registers a debt to the older poet.[3] My grouping of these poets makes no pretense to any authority other than my own sense of literary history and taste. Certainly, other poets could be brought in—Robert Creeley and Galway Kinnell, for example, or the Irish poet, Seamus Heaney—who, like Roethke, celebrates the kingdom of bang and blab—and, as well, the American poets, David Wagoner, John Logan, and Roland Flint, who have all benefited from Roethke; to this extent, however, my grouping must remain arbitrary. The variety of achievement represented by the poets I have chosen suggests striking differences rather than similarities between them, differences that from the start would place James Wright and James Dickey in opposite camps. Because a Roethkean mode is evident in the work of these poets, I have used that mode as a criterion to distinguish between them. Consequently, I have sometimes yielded to the temptation of evaluating these poets out of a sense of deference to the master, Roethke, but perhaps sometimes unconsciously out of my own errant whim. The Roethkean edge defining that delicate balance between the perfection of personality and the perfection of its surrender becomes, in turn, the point of balance for these poets. Not all of these poets stay near the edge, and two of them, it seems to me, avoid it in their own respective ways, despite their implied recognition of it. Of course, none of these poets are merely imitating Roethke; there does not seem to be any conscious copying of style—yet in adapting Roethke (there is no parody and impersonation) to their ends there is some carry-over in style, especially in some of the poetry of James Wright. More important, however, it is to the kinship in theme and purpose that I have addressed myself.

Accordingly, I have grouped James Wright and Robert Bly together because they both share Roethke's repugnance for a high-speed, technocratic society in their poetry, a poetry that strives for an insistence on a personal but archetypal autonomy as a prelude to their animistic themes. James Dickey, by his own choosing, remains a singular figure in attempting to employ Roethke's animism to his own individual needs. Sylvia Plath and Ted Hughes obviously belong together because their poetry represents complementary modes of experience that could be said to derive its force from much of Roethke's sense of animism and tragic inevitability. Indeed, these two poets might be viewed as Roethke's lost children, the one engaging the suicidal journey in search of a father, the other having survived that journey at some cost.

Adjusting from Outrage: James Wright and Robert Bly

Anyone reading through James Wright's *Collected Poems*[4] will readily note a change of style in the volume beginning the second half of the collection, *The Branch Will Not Break*. The preceding pages record a number of traditional verse forms from the rhyming couplet to the sonnet that give way in the second half almost entirely to a Roethkean lyrical mode, adapting his kind of verse and intuitive nature imagery. Here is an example that is a skillful adaptation of a Roethkean image from "The Rose" ("Was it here I wore a crown of birds for a moment"):

> I step into the water
> Of two flakes.
> The crowns of white birds rise
> To my ankles,
> To my knees,
> To my face.
>
> "Snowstorm in the Midwest" (*WCP*, 130)

It can be recognized at once as the Roethkean mode: the unmasked poet speaking with the urgency of an intense moment in the actual present, the slow verbal rhythms, the oppressiveness of the "birds" image creating the sense of an animistic merging with nature. Wright is a poet who has absorbed his influences, however, and there is evident everywhere in the poetry a compulsion to perfect, even to protect that achievement, which presupposes an identity worth protecting, like "The Jewel" (echoing Roethke's "The Adamant"):

> There is this cave
> In the air behind my body
> That nobody is going to touch:
> A cloister, a silence
> Closing around a blossom of fire.
>
> (*WCP*, 114)

Yet with Wright's change of style midway through his collection, there is really no change of subject; no new themes are introduced, rather it is those themes of his earlier volumes, especially the third part of *Saint Judas*, "The Part Nearest Home," that are continued throughout the collection, perfecting Wright's peculiar tone. The reader finds, for example, the celebration of the criminal in the poem to Caryl Chessman, and this declared affinity with the criminal mind—one that Roethke himself shared[5]—suggests by a simple irony Wright's attitude toward American society as being itself criminal:

> Those deer on the hillside have no idea what in hell
> We are except murderers.
> They know that much, and don't think
> They don't.
>
>   (*WCP*, 185)

Wright takes Roethke's pessimism a step further in the direction of anarchy, unmindful of resisting the disease he sees, like "Stages on a Journey Westward," repeating the Roethkean journey westward and using it as a trope for outrage:

> I lie down between tombstones.
> At the bottom of the cliff
> America is over and done with.
> America,
> Plunged into the dark furrows
> Of the sea again.
>
>   (*WCP*, 117)

The last three lines could be a wish rather than an indictment, a wish for unconscious submergence and ultimately a rebirth, and this submergence might begin with the individual, Wright himself. Thus, the Roethkean *I*, the archetypal voice, unequivocally establishes itself as a singular voice, conditioned only by the minimal, place of birth and parent:

> My name is James A. Wright, and I was born
> Twenty-five miles from this infected grave,
> In Martins Ferry, Ohio, where one slave
> To Hazel-Atlas Glass became my father.
>
> (*WCP*, 82)

In these solemn, measured lines from *Saint Judas*, Wright's obsessive theme emerges: learning to die: "I do not pity the dead, I pity the dying" (*WCP*, 83). Roethke's theme of learning to die, as has been traced in the three major poems, invokes a world of process very much involved with the sense of place in the poet's life, both his memory of places and of present surroundings. It is as if place is the only means of learning available to the poet to structure an identity with which to die, for place itself is dying (Woodlawn or Oyster River); this sense of place informs Wright's poetry as well: "Dying's the best/ Of all the arts men learn in a dead place" (*WCP*, 82). Perhaps Wright had Roethke in mind in these lines; at any rate it is clear that Wright sees America as a dead place, a wasteland, a place to be pitied, really:

> Pity so old and alone, it is not alone, yours or mine,
> The pity of rivers and children, the pity of brothers,
>   the pity
> Of our country, which is our lives.
>
> (*WCP*, 212)

The arch criminal for a Christian society is, of course, Judas, Christ's betrayer, but for Wright, Judas is a saint because society, in effect, has condemned him, a figure without hope, and for Wright, therefore, a figure of pity:

> Then I remembered bread my flesh had eaten,
> The kiss that ate my flesh. Flayed without hope,
> I held the man for nothing in my arms.
>
> *(WCP*, 85).

Even in *New Poems*, the last section of the collected edition, Wright still refers to his dead hero ("I dream of my poor Judas walking along and alone" *WCP*, 173). Such poems as "A Prayer to Escape the Market Place," "Gambling in Stateline Nevada," "Before a Cashier's Window in a Department Store," and "A Way to Make a Living" effectively transpose the Judas-crime over to the state, America as betrayer. In the last poem mentioned, Wright delineates the issue in terms of death, caring for the dead, and he chooses not to inhabit the graveyard of, "Grocers and judges, the polished/ Dead of whom we make/ So much":

> Thank you, no.
> I am going to take my last nourishment
> Of measure from a dark blue
> Ripple on swell on ripple that makes
> Its own garlands.
>
> *(WCP*, 192)

Following in much the same manner as Roethke, Wright's proposal is to recover "lost" beginnings from the dead, from the past. The symbol for this recovery throughout much of his poetry is the small, the diminutive, and like Roethke he takes his measure from nature, a "measure from a dark blue/ Ripple," "a little ripple of rain/ Or a small waterfall" *(WCP*, 209). It is in Wright's poetry of learning to die that the Roethkean strain of keeping in touch with the minimal comes into focus. Consider the poem "I Was Af-

raid of Dying," which is done very much in the Roethkean
lyrical manner with its peculiar diction, imagery, uneven
line lengths, present tense, and participles all working to
dramatize the speaker's ascendancy from fear:

> Once,
> I was afraid of dying
> In a field of dry weeds.
> But now,
> All day long I have been walking among damp fields,
> Trying to keep still, listening
> To insects that move patiently.
> Perhaps they are sampling the fresh dew that gathers
>   slowly
> In empty snail shells
> And in the secret shelters of sparrow feathers fallen on
>   the earth.
>
> (*WCP*, 134)

And also in the ending of "The Minneapolis Poem," Wright
renounces his live burial in Minneapolis, and with an im-
ploring tone, recalling the prayers of Roethke's old woman,
begs God for release, which, if one were not familiar with
the outrage of Wright's sincerity, might simply degenerate
into embarrassment for the reader:

> I want to be lifted up
> By some great white bird unknown to the police,
> And soar for a thousand miles and be carefully hidden
> Modest and golden as one last corn grain,
> Stored with the secrets of the wheat and the mysterious
>   lives
> Of the unnamed poor.
>
> (*WCP*, 141)

In Wright's angry search for identity ("I am lost in the
beautiful white ruins/ Of America" *WCP*, 132) one always

comes upon the pervading strains of animism ("A horse grazes in my long shadow" *WCP*, 130), and there is always that peculiar honesty that Wright manages (a fine achievement for any contemporary writing at a time when the thorns of irony are always threatening), and that is perhaps best exemplified in the well-known poem about the blue jay: "for he knows as well as I do/ The branch will not break" (*WCP*, 125). It is difficult to see how an intensely animistic poem like the equally well-known "A Blessing" could have been written without the Roethkean model preceding it. Wright's affection for an Indian pony in this particular poem is dramatically convincing ("There is no loneliness like theirs" *WCP*, 135) with the sudden realization of a spirit within him as he caresses the pony's ear: "if I stepped out of my body I would break/ Into blossom." And it is "the young tufts of spring in the darkness" that the ponies are munching all the while that reinforces the animism binding animal and man.

Following the Roethkean model, Wright is mindful of a shaping spirit hunting form and definition, and the converse of this process as well. Many of Wright's poems invoke woman as spirit, in the same way Roethke did (*see* "Words for the Wind"), because the female is identified as being closer to her origins, her natural beginnings, than her male counterpart, like "Trying to Pray" that speaks for a furtive joy shimmering somewhere between "women's hands" and the "leaves" of a tree:

> It is the good darkness
> Of women's hands that touch loaves.
> The spirit of a tree begins to move.
> I touch leaves.
> I close my eyes and think of water.

> (*WCP*, 128, 129)

The tone and imagery of the last two lines are pure
Roethke. Other poems written in the Roethkean mode are
"Fear is What Quickens Me," "A Secret Gratitude," "A
Poem About Breasts," "Beginning," "Echo for the Promise
of George Trakl's Life," parts six and seven of "Many of
Our Waters," "Poems to a Brown Cricket," and "A Moral
Poem Freely Accepted from Sappho." I would like, however, to quote in full the poem, "Beginning," because it
brings together much of what has been discussed so far, and
it succeeds, as does the best of Roethke's poetry written in
this manner, for the attention given to particularity and
distinctiveness, rather than synthesis and fusion:

> The moon drops one or two feathers into the field.
> The dark wheat listens.
> Be still.
> Now.
> There they are, the moon's young, trying
> Their wings.
> Between trees, a slender woman lifts up the lovely
>   shadow
> Of her face, and now she steps into the air, now she is
>   gone
> Wholly, into the air.
> I stand alone by an elder tree, I do not dare breathe
> Or move.
> I listen.
> The wheat leans back towards its own darkness.
> And I lean toward mine.
>
> (*WCP*, 127)

Here Wright describes the processes of dying for both man
and nature about as forcefully and honestly as any contemporary poet could hope for; the present is obsessively present, enhancing the sense of "beginning," as well as release,

of letting the woman go "wholly" into the air, like the Yeatsian swan that disappears in spite of itself. It is the real sense of death and life that the poet creates in the poem that creates, too, his separate identity, no less important—and certainly no more important—than the wheat itself. Wright, too, is journeying out of the self because he knows, like Roethke, that, "The self-seeker finds nothing" (*WCP*, 113), particularly in a society that both fondles and exploits the self-seeker as an economic necessity.

As I mentioned earlier, Wright has absorbed his influences, having shown his own particular metermaking argument that derives its strengths from a close attention paid to verbal precision and sound forms employing much assonance and consonance. Yeats has said, "We begin to live when we have conceived life as tragedy,"[6] and it would seem both Roethke and Wright bear out this belief in their poetry—their breath-controlled lines and their meditative moods engendering at times a hard-earned optimism. As the younger poet, Wright carries the increasing burden of influence of the poets who precede him, and using Roethke's almost unprecedented sense of abreaction (not necessarily confessional) in his role of an unmasked speaker (and one thinks, too, of Eliot's voice in "Gerontion": "I would meet you upon this honestly"), he thanks his "friends," and at the same time acknowledges his own independence:

> All this time I've been slicking into my own words
> The beautiful language of my friends.
> I have to use my own, now.
> That's why this scattering poem sounds the way it does.
> (*WCP*, 212)

As an editor and a translator, in addition to writing poetry, Robert Bly has become in his own way an unannounced spokesman for a Roethkean kind of poetry, and at the same time an announced spokesman for an American poetry of the imagination released from the history of Western ideas. The new poetry is to direct itself to the deep images of the unconscious, borrowing its method from the French (Rimbaud, Eluard, Char), the Spanish (Machado, Vallejo, Jimenez, Lorca), and the German (Rilke, Trakl, Benn), and avoiding as much as possible the English tradition in poetry that has become too abstract for Bly's taste.[7] Iambic pentameter must give way to a free verse in which poets can carry on "a sustained raid into modern life"; thus, a successful poem for Bly would require the poet's imagination to operate in three realms: "the dark figures of politics, the world of streetcars, and the ocean world."[8] Bly praises the life of solitude for the poet, for only in solitude can the poet voyage into the unconscious as the French have done (ironically, the ghosts of Blake, Wordsworth, Shelley, and Keats must be looking over Bly's shoulder), a voyage few Americans have been willing to take, except for Whitman, Crane, and Roethke, who have contributed to the "little genuine poetry we have."[9]

I would like to say a few words about Bly's prose before turning to the poetry because what he has to say, particularly about politics and poetry in America, is extremely interesting with regard to Roethke's poetry. Bly's position is perhaps an unpopular one, given his attempt to throttle the establishment in American letters by passing off such poets as Ransom, Jarrell, Lowell, Whittemore, Snodgrass, even Creeley, as merely personal poets (Whittemore and Nemerov, in particular, are foils to Bly's interests).[10] Much like Roethke before him, Bly sees a link between the spirit of a nation, its national psyche, and the psyche of the poet, that is, the poet who goes beyond the personal, the ego, into the archetypal and impersonal depths of the unconscious (the void for schooling the spirit, which is America). Bly elaborates this position convincingly, I think, when he speaks of an entangled sharing going on between the really good poem that journeys out of the self and a larger psyche that can be called a nation's life. Paraphrasing Yeats, Bly says, "A true political poem is a quarrel with ourselves, and the rhetoric is as harmful in that sort of poem as in the personal poem. The true political poem does not order us either to take any specific acts: like the personal poem, it moves to deepen awareness."[11] With these aims in mind, Bly edited an anthology of poems, *Forty Poems Touching on Recent American History* (1970), intending to penetrate into the psyche of the nation, and to give rise then to an imaginatively induced psychic picture of the United States. Again, one is reminded of the English Romantics with their political interests operating as a primary source to much of the imagination in their poetry. In his preface, Bly wisely pays his respects to otherwise alien poets, Pound and Eliot, who revived true political poetry for a brief spell in American letters: "Pound demanded that American history enter his *Cantos*, Eliot wrote well, though always of a generalized modern nation, rather than of the U.S."[12] Whitman, of course, initiated this mode of political poetry, after which it became dormant until the generation of Pound and Eliot. Bly includes Roethke's "Night Journey" that should immediately tell the reader of the apolitical nature (in the nonpartisan sense) of Bly's purpose. Ideally, empire follows art, as Blake has said, and it is this ideal that is kept in focus when Bly speaks of a poetry, not of political opinion, but of psychic growth journeying out of the self. Roethke, too, embraced this ideal when he spoke of his intuitive approach to "The Lost Son" and its related poems: "Several people have made the point that they [the poems] are at once a personal history and a history of the race itself . . . . I can make no claim, of course, one way or another."[13] Roethke's last sentence only emphasizes the intuitive ground of reference.

So far it is quite apparent that Bly is bordering on Freudian and Jungian ideas of the unconscious, and it is no surprise to later find him referring to these two thinkers in a prose piece included in his latest volume of poetry, *Sleepers Joining Hands* (1973). In a careful outline of his purpose as a writer, Bly also refers to Neumann (*The Great Mother*), in addition to Freud and Jung, and he sets about praising the anima, the feminine soul, acknowledging further the matriarchal origins of all societies (hence the need to go back into the unconscious) and their demise, as well, by a rebellious patriarchy, causing then an imbalance between the feminine and masculine souls to the general detriment of society, especially Western society (one might add that the reader need only look to the *Odyssey* to see the crisis dramatized in terms of the "feminine" first half of the poem in which Odysseus is essentially wandering through his unconscious, and the second "masculine" half in which, as a returning husband, he restores order in Ithaca). Bly's remarks are sweeping, but reasoned, and seem to speak for what is essentially a Roethkean kind of poetry. I think it worth quoting his remarks about righting the "spiritual balance," as he puts it, because of his excerpts from Jung and their close kinship to Roethke's position:

> Jung, whose father was a Protestant minister, said: "The intellect has achieved the most tremendous things, but all that time our spiritual house has been falling to pieces . . . . Meaning has left most religious images . . . . And I am convinced that this growing impoverishment of symbols has a meaning . . . . And if we hide our nakedness, as the Theosophists do, by putting on the gorgeous robes and trappings of the

East, we are essentially lying about our own history. It would be far better to admit our spiritual poverty.... The spirit has come down from its fiery high places ... but when spirit becomes heavy, it turns to water.... Therefore the way of the soul in search of its lost father ... leads to the water, to the dark mirror that lies at the bottom. Whoever has decided to move toward the state of spiritual poverty ... goes the way of the soul that leads to the water."

I see in my own poems and the poems of so many other poets alive now fundamental attempts to right our own spiritual balance, by encouraging those parts in us that are linked with music, with solitude, water, and trees, the parts that grow when we are far from the centers of ambition.[14]

What Jung speaks of here corresponds to Roethke's so-called Papa principle; Roethke, as a lost son aware of his spiritual impoverishment, searches for the parent and eventually, or symbolically, for the primal parent, or parents, in order to restore the spiritual balance between parents and child within the memory of the living. This spiritual balance involves a psychic balance having archetypal implications reflected both in a nation's history and the individual's. In "The Lost Son," as will be remembered, Roethke refers to both primal parents ("Rub me in father and mother"), with the patriarchal note sounded in the lines: "Fear was my father, Father Fear./ His look drained the stones," and the matriarchal in the lines: "I want the old rage, the lash of primordial milk!/ Goodbye, goodbye, old stones, the time order is going." If one equates stones (admittedly an ambivalent symbol) with the feminine soul or a matriarchal order rather than a masculine (sphericity, of course, is a traditionally feminine quality), then the line, "His look drained the stones," evinces a spiritual imbalance within that particular context.

I do not mean to suggest that Roethke is consciously praising either the feminine or the masculine, but that he is concerned only with dramatizing a conflict between the two. The conflict itself is a source of ambivalence that is certainly manifest in the poetry. It would be difficult, if not misleading, to characterize Roethke's search after a spiritual balance as favoring one order over another, as Bly does, because in addition to Roethke's praise of the feminine order as a "jauntier principle of order" in "Meditations of an Old Woman," and his plea for protection ("Mnetha, Mother of Har, protect me") in "North American Sequence," there is the deference to the masculine toward the end of that sequence although, as has been pointed out, subtly qualified by the feminine. What is important is that a sense of order and balance between the masculine and the feminine is restored in the poet's mind, a result in keeping, certainly, with Bly's own purpose as he states it.

Turning now to Bly's poetry, one might wonder just what kind of poetry to expect from a writer who shows a kind of Poundian energy in attempting to derail the establishment. Curiously enough, there seems to be a similarity between the two when one compares Bly's later poems to the prosy style of *The Cantos*: there is that sharp, serrated edge to his style, an explosive quality that, obsessed with extending the themes of his prose, favors a dogmatic, sometimes desperate tone that is too often self-conscious to pass for the best in lyrical poetry:

> The mind waters run out on the rug.
> Pull the mind in,
> pull the arm in,
> it will be taken off by a telephone post.[15]

Or the following lines from the same volume:

> When the waterholes go, and the fish flop about
> in the caked mud, they can moisten each other faintly.
>   That is good, but best
> is to let them lose themselves in a river.[16]

What these lines show is a disregard for the syllabic life of the language in their attempt to advance the poet's rhetoric, that is, to engage in a specific act rather than deepen the reader's awareness. Imagery becomes confused because there is a lack of contextual background to support the imagery ("rug" and "telephone post," in the first example) either on a deep or surface level. In the second example, several words merely dangle rather than function: "go," "about," "faintly," "best," and the idea that fish can lose themselves seems to contradict Bly's purpose, for it is the reader who is lost or losing himself; the fish continually discovers itself in the river, an idea inherent in the line from the adjacent poem: "I am ashamed looking at the fish in the water."

As Roethke has said in "Meditations of an Old Woman": "There are no pursuing forms" for modern man, and it would appear that Bly has this thought in mind as he moves the mind's spotlight through the deep waters of the unconscious, searching for form. Nothing in the way of imagery is spared; to be selective is to admit a "fear of the unconscious," thus betraying that trust in the unconscious that the French insisted on (notwithstanding the excesses of Dadaism).[17] Certainly Bly's intentions are pure, but that of course does not mean the poetry is. With all this zeal given over to ferreting out the deep image, there is bound to emerge some meaningless jargon, yet there are times when the poetry is imaginatively right, when image and context are mutually supportive, like the following stanza:

> A woman whispers to me, urges me to speak truths.
> "I am afraid that you won't be honest with me."
> Half or more of the moon rolls on in shadow.
> Owls talk at night, loons wheel cries through lower
>   waters,
> Fragments of the mother lie open in all low places.[18]

Bly's choice of words is precise, giving rise to unending shades of suggestion that reverberate within the stanza's meaning summed up in the last line where the rhythms finally fall under the trochee's heave. Roethke's, "The ear hears only in low places" (*CP*, 59), comes to mind as well.

A few years earlier in the volume, *The Light Around the Body* (1967), one finds many good poems playing on Roethkean themes, as even suggested by the section titles: "The Two Worlds," "In Praise of Grief," "A Body Not Yet Born."[19] And Bly explicitly points to one of these themes, exhibiting, like Wright, an honesty rooted in outrage: "That is why these poems are so sad/ The long dead running over the fields."[20] Bly's journey out of the self is down to the "low places"; the reader never arrives, of course, because, "We are still falling," as he says in one of his many poems about journeying, "A Journey with Women." Place is as important to Bly as it is to Roethke because it is where the struggle for identity begins: "those roads in South Dakota that feel around in the darkness."[21] If one is still falling, it is because he has not awakened, like Roethke's lost son, to "A second life" through a "nourishment in death"; but it is the deep imagery of the unconscious that does awake the reader and stops his fall, sending him then upward, free from fear, like the rising spirit of Roethke's old woman:

In the deep fall, the body awakes,
And we find lions on the seashore—
Nothing to fear.
The wind rises, the water is born.[22]

In the adjacent poem to the one I have been quoting from,
Bly draws a timely contrast, for here there is an absence of
motion, a scene only of stiff shapes that the falling snow
accents as it, too, comes to stillness and death: "It rests on
the doorsills of collapsing children's houses,/ And on transformer boxes held from the ground forever in the center of
cornfields." Unmoving, above the ground, or "low places,"
the transformer box is Bly's image for spiritless man (or
Roethke's "self-involved") held forever from the ground,
unable to slip like Roethke's vital sense of spirit "just under
the water."

Bly's journey usually begins from an acute sense of present time and place that acts as a kind of springboard into
memory where "the dumb shall speak," a Roethkean history of the psyche, as these lines reveal:

Walks in large cities late at night,
Or reading the Bible in Christian Science windows,
Or reading a history of Bougainville.
Then the images appear:
Images of death,
Images of the body shaken in the grave,
And the graves filled with seawater;
Fires in the sea,
The ships smouldering like bodies,
Images of wasted life,
Life lost, imagination ruined,
The house fallen,
The gold sticks broken,
Then shall the talkative be silent,
And the dumb shall speak.[23]

Going back further in time to Bly's first volume, *Silence in the Snowy Fields* (1962), one finds more of the same crafts-manship in terms of tone and balance, more of those Roethkean themes: the sense of place as beginning, a seek-ing after low places, and an identification of life with and through death:

> Lincoln's statue, and the traffic. From the long past
> Into the long present
> A bird, forgotten in these pressures, warbling,
> As the great wheel turns around, grinding
> The living in water.
> Washing, continual washing, in water now stained
> With blossoms and rotting logs,
> Cries, half-muffled, from beneath the earth, the living
>   awakened at last like the dead.[24]

Names of places abound, from Minnesota to Maryland, and there is usually some sudden (*suddenly* is a favorite word for Bly) revelation or deepening awareness when the right image is used, like the last two lines of "Driving Toward the Lac Qui Parle River": "When I reach the river, the full moon covers it;/ A few people are talking low in a boat."[25]

In keeping ideology out of his poetry, Bly often invokes the animistic, in the same way as Roethke does ("Inside me there is a confusion of swallows,/ Birds flying through the smoke"[26]). But this sense of animism, as seen with Roethke sometimes, can be easily transformed into a death-wish, and not necessarily death as nourishment; for example, in the poem "Depression":

> Now I want to go back among the dark roots;
> Now I want to see the day pulling its long wing;
> I want to see nothing more than two feet high;
> I want to see no one, I want to say nothing,
> I want to go down and rest in the black earth of
> silence.[27]

The will to animism releases, however, a shaping spirit that hunts some bodily form, and it is this belief that motivates the poet into writing:

> I know that far out in the Minnesota lake
> Fish are nosing the mouths of cold springs,
> Whose water causes ripples in the sleeping sand,
> Like a spirit moving in a body.[28]

It would seem fair to say that Bly, like Wright, intensifies Roethke's disenchantment with society and its archsymbol, the institution, that this disenchantment has become almost a revulsion giving rise to the prophetic voice of doom, tentative at best: "America is still young herself, and she may become something magnificent and shining, or she may turn, as Rome did, into a black dinosaur, the enemy of every nation in the world who wants to live its own life. In my opinion, that decision has not been made."[29]

The Egotistical Sublime: James Dickey

> I, who came back from the depths laughing too loudly,
> Become another thing;
> My eyes extend beyond the farthest bloom of the
>   waves;
> I lose and find myself in the long water;
> I am gathered together once more;
> I embrace the world.

That is what we want: to be gathered together once more, to be able to enter in, to participate in experience, to possess our lives. I think that the new poetry will be a poetry of the dazzling simple statement . . . .[30]

James Dickey's air-borne praise of Roethke—he refers to him as the greatest American poet America has ever had—is by now well known, and his quotation above from Roethke's "The Long Waters" would indicate to readers that he is impressed with Roethke's expansive embrace of universals, a rebirth from the depths into "another thing." It is just this kind of regenerative expansiveness that characterizes so much of Dickey's own poetry, especially his later poetry from *Buckdancer's Choice* (1965) to *The Eye Beaters, Blood, Victory, Madness, Buckhead, and Mercy* (1970). Dickey is aware, of course, that Roethke is a poet of the self, as Dickey considers himself to be, yet it is Dickey's particular ideas of self that clearly distinguish him from his contemporaries and, ironically, from much of Roethke. That Dickey intends himself to be a solitary figure in American poetry— assuming something of a Whitmanesque stance—is evident from his summary dismissal of the four other poets being considered here.[31] Again, it is somewhat ironic that Roethke's most self-expressed admirer is the poet who shows the least influence, that is, he has not absorbed his influence, but rather has remained merely derivative for the most part.

If Roethke has concerned himself with the long journey out of the self (who, like Bloom in *Ulysses*, knows that the longest way around is the shortest way home), then Dickey has concerned himself with the unparadoxical opposite: "a really great poem goes *straight* to it."[32] Sublimity, intensity, vision, all without paradox, all contribute to an expansive form of expression: "The poem is a window opening not on truth but on possibility for dramatic expression that may well come to *be* what we think of as truth."[33] Much of Dickey's poetry expresses an explosion of personality, multiple *I*'s (each poem an expression of a different *I* figure) in an attempt to facet the given personality of the poet. What happens in Dickey's case, however, is that the poet's identity is not faceted or defined in terms of the other—as it is in Roethke's "North American Sequence," for example—rather, it is diffused through the anecdotal qualities of the poem, returning only to what was originally given: an ego in need of expression. The journey out of the self nourishes the self, redefines it; the return to the self via the poem, or poems, is never quite back to the point or level of origin—there is some development in the human condition for better or worse. Perhaps Dickey has this romantic notion in mind when he speaks for a possibility of dramatic expression, but too often he journeys into the realm of the impossible from which there is no return, and hence the human dimension is lost. In some of the more well-known poems I find this to be the case. In "The Heaven of Animals," an anthologized piece, there is this going "straight" to the matter, but there is no conviction, no dramatic awareness exhibited by the poet speaking for these animals:

> Under such trees in full knowledge
> Of what is in glory above them,
> And to feel no fear,
> But acceptance, compliance.
> Fulfilling themselves without pain.[34]

What human possibilities can arise from this impossible human assertion of a painless existence for animals? In "Springer Mountain" the dramatic possibilities fail in a scene where man confronts the animal world (a characteristic theme in Dickey, having obvious roots in Roethke) only to conclude rather blandly that it will be the first and last time the poet will hunt deer. The clothes-changing or nude scene is more gesture than action (an overly contrived, pretentious action) and does not come off as a determinant to what otherwise should be a foregone conclusion.

"Reincarnation (I)" takes the animistic theme to its limits, insuring, therefore, no return—no *convincing* return— to the human realm. In this case a man assumes the identity of a snake: "Fallen from that estate, he has gone down on his knees/ And beyond, disappearing into the egg buried under the sand" (*DCP*, 196). The poem follows through with what amounts to a "straight" description of the animal realm with the last line attempting to bring the reader back through the simile, "like a county judge striking a match," which is simply not enough. And in the later poem, "The Sheep Child," there is the rhetorical shove to get the poem moving on a firmer ground of possibility (here the speaker is the sheep child):

> Dead, I am most surely living
> In the minds of farm boys: I am he who drives
> Them like wolves from the hound bitch and calf
> And from the chaste ewe in the wind.
>
> (*DCP*, 253)

But for the most part the poem is too far into the realm of impossibility to give it a redirection into human possibility. Even the famous "The Firebombing," a less rhetorical, less theatrical performance than is usual for Dickey, diffuses its compelling theme of guilt in the closing couplet: "Absolution? Sentence? No matter;/ The thing itself is in that" (*DCP*, 188).

Guilt is a major theme in Dickey's poetry, a theme that arises from two facts in the poet's life that he has expressly made a record of, namely, the death of an older brother upon which Dickey's own birth depended, and his survival as a combat fighter-pilot in two wars.[35] In each case there attaches a personal sense of guilt for merely being alive under these circumstances, and it is understandable that Dickey, like Roethke before him, should try to fashion a

poetic that metaphorically confronts death as an appease-
ment, a therapy even, for the poet's feelings of guilt. As has
been seen in the case of Roethke, invoking the animistic in
one's poetry is to invoke a death-wish as well:

> I would delight in my hands, the branch singing, alter-
> ing the excessive bird;
> I long for the imperishable quiet at the heart of form;
> I would be a stream, winding between great striated
> rocks in late summer;
> A leaf, I would love the leaves, delighting in the redo-
> lent disorder of this mortal life,
> This ambush, this silence.
>
> "The Longing"

In other words, there is a risk to be taken in invoking the
animistic, and this risk, that of surrendering identity altogether, must be given expression to complete the theme,
to render it human. Dickey does not go the distance; he asserts his animism rather than creates a real sense of merging that Roethke is able to do. Dickey's kind of animism, his
romantic sense of reincarnation, is a kind of wish fulfillment that often confuses art with life ("I am sick of self-
effacing poetry. It is time we got some glory back into it"[36]).
Such a poetry will always hold out hope in one form or
another, or possibilities, to use Dickey's term (*see*, for example, "The Escape" *DCP*, 203). But to go for glory is risky
even for Dickey: "Anyone who courts sublimity has to run
the risk of looking ridiculous."[37] The ridiculous, however,
does not reside in the impossible: impossible dreams, impossible hopes, impossible glory that passes for so much
surface glitter of daily life that is the shimmering facade for
those underlying realities of guilt—personal, familial, and
archetypal. The ridiculous is more apt to be the reality of
the waste-sad time stretching before and after, and of the

right image plunging into that waste and still surviving. Too often, Dickey's words are weakly abstract and merely hold up that facade of hope and glory, and for that reason they lack an edge or point with which to penetrate the mind or psyche; here are some, for example, gleaned from the entire spectrum of his poetry: gold, heaven, king, pure, holy, true, truly, world, angel, sovereign, glory, amazed, marvelous, glorious, deadly, richest, deepest, softest, vast, flashing, great. It is perhaps unfair of me to pick at random, but the relative ease with which one can choose these abstractions and superlatives indicates in itself their recurring pattern in the poetry. It is this penchant for generalizing, too, that keeps the poetry relatively free from symbolic imagery, that is, the deep image, allowing it to employ, rather, a decorative use of simile intending to serve the narrative and anecdotal form of the poem. Perhaps it would do well to refer to some of Dickey's remarks on his kind of poetry before returning to the subject of imagery; he speaks here of modes of poetry he has developed or is developing:

> I have three modes of poetry that I am working in now. One is the narrative-dramatic mode that most of my work heretofore has been in. Second is the so-called "new metric." The third, the one I have done least writing in and least experimentation in, is what I call "country surrealism. . . ." A fourth possibility is translation work and *mis*readings, from, say the German . . . . Another mode is the mode in which I wrote the "Pine" poems. That would give me five.[38]

In all these possible modes, however, the narrative element remains strong, and the sense of action always seems to be foremost in the poet's mind. Dickey is so concerned about action in his poetry that the metaphorical and symbolical significance of the imagery becomes subordinated, if not neglected:

I want more than anything else, for the poem to be an experience—that is, a physical experience—for the reader. It must be completed action, and the plunging in of the reader into this action is the most difficult and the most desirable feat that the poet can perform. Nothing can be more important than this: it is the difference between poetry of reflection and poetry of participation. It may not restore the soul, but it restores the body.[39]

How different from Roethke's remarks about his *Praise to the End!* sequence:

Much of the action is implied . . . . The revelation of the identity of the speaker may itself be a part of the drama; or, in some instances, in a dream sequence, his identity may emerge with someone else's, or be deliberately blurred. This struggle for spiritual identity is, of course, one of the perpetual recurrences. (This is not the same as the flight of the adolescent personality for recognition in the "real" world.) Disassociation often precedes a new state of clarity.

(*SP*, 41)

Because the image is so important for Roethke ("to telescope image and symbol" *SP*, 42), one should turn to what Dickey calls his fifth mode in which he uses an "associational imagery of a very special and wide ranging sort [that] can be applied to subjects either small or large, short or long. The thing may have tremendous depth and suggestibility. But I don't understand it yet."[40] A look at some of the lines in "Pine" will show what Dickey means by his "associational imagery." As an example of his new mode, this poem is not unlike his earlier work, such as the two "Reincarnation" poems, "Inside the River," "The Being," "Approaching Prayer," among others, that show a strong narrative on the animistic theme. In fact, this mode might simply be called a narrative animism in which the speaker in the poem most usually assumes the identity (or asserts that identity) of the animal or nonhuman object and proceeds to describe the event or experience in somewhat sensationalist terms, rhetorically designed to suggest feelings of awe (I quote from the last two sections):

IV

More hands on the terrible rough.
More pain but more than all
Is lodged in the leg-insides. More holding,
Though, more swaying, Rise and ride
Like this and wear and ride
Away with a passionate faceful
Of ply and points. The whole thing turns
On earth, throwing off a dark
Flood of four ways
Of being here blind and bending
Blacked-out and framed
Suspended and found alive in the rough palm—
And thigh-fires of friction, embracing in the beyond
It all, where,
Opening one by one, you can still open
One thing more. A final form
And color at last comes out
Of you alone putting it all
Together like nothing
Here like Almighty

V
Glory.[41]

Compared to his earlier work there is more of a clipped movement to the lines, but the narrative is still strong, a straight description really, using connecting (associative in the literal sense) imagery that is not deep ("with a passionate faceful/ Of ply and points"). For Dickey the narrative itself is the image, perhaps intended to be a deep image or, in other words, the poem itself as metaphor, but if such be the case, the poem fails to define a medium in which to plunge as an image or metaphor; there is only the suggestion of impossibility (which is always possibility for Dickey) from which there is no return.

Dickey's best poetry is that which comes to grips with the baffling subjects of guilt and sex, and their interrelationship. Here he manages to fashion a mythic quality that makes for a genuinely honest response, a deepening awareness of the human condition, like "The Enclosure," with its themes of sexual repression under wartime conditions:

> as from women
> Sleeping kept from themselves, and beyond me,
> To sweat as I did, to the north:
> To pray to a skylight of paper, and fall
> On the enemy's women
> With intact and incredible love.
>
> (*DCP*, 27)

or "Cherrylog Road" with its dramatization of illicit love ambiguously dependent from guilt ("with no trace of me on her face/ To be seen by her red-haired father" *DCP*, 136), a sexual love made all the more transient, yet valuable, by the surrounding death of the junkyard. "The Fiend" is another such poem in which Dickey explores with consummate understanding sexual repression in an urban setting. I would add, too, some of those poems that treat the animistic theme with a sense of detachment, allowing the merger between human and animal to evolve from the poem, like Roethke's "The Lost Son," particularly the animal world of the opening section, and the vegetal or floral world of the closing section (and also Roethke's short poems: "Snake," "The Lizard," "The Pike," "The Meadow Mouse," "The Geranium")—such poems as: "The Dusk of Horses," "A Screen Porch in the Country," "To His Children in Darkness," "The Owl King," and "The Movement of Fish."

As a poet attempting the Roethkean mode, Dickey presents a too personal manner to perfect that mode. The journey out of the self is dramatized, rather, by an acute auditory sense and verbal precision that selects an imagery for penetrating the psyche. "I know something about the pure clear word," says James Wright,

> Though I am not yet a grown man.
> And who is he?
>
> The long body of his dream is the beginning of a dark
> Hair under an illiterate
> Girl's ear.
>
> And everybody goes on explaining to us
> The difference between a nutmeg and a squirrel,
> The grown man plows down.
>
> (*WCP*, 208, 209)

There is a directness here, not unlike that sense of immediacy, perhaps "Dazzling" simplicity that Dickey calls for, which contributes, certainly, to a narrative form, but imbedded in this narrative matrix is the striking image ("a dark/ Hair under an illiterate/ Girl's ear") that seeks out the limits of resonance with the surrounding lines, the surrounding narrative matrix. Too often in Dickey's poetry there is an absence of this kind of tension between imagery and narrative, and more often there is only rhetoric imposed upon the narrative:

Gun down
The engines, the eight blades sighing
For the moment when the roofs will connect
Their flames, and make a town burning with all
American fire.
                              Reflections of houses catch;
Fire shuttles from pond to pond
In every direction, till hundreds flash with one death.
With this in the dark of the mind,
Death will not be what it should;
Will not, even now, even when
My exhaled face in the mirror
Of bars, dilates in a cloud like Japan.

(DCP, 185)

The Lost Children: Sylvia Plath and Ted Hughes

Sylvia Plath's poetry derives much of its force from the darker side of Roethke, extending the Roethkean journey by means of her verbal precision and almost clotted sense of imagery until the fusion between art and life was completed in her suicide. Unlike Dickey, Plath saw no reason to celebrate the ego by voicing an all-pervasive animism. Her animism is more like Wright's, a way of learning to die, and to this extent she is closer to Roethke's lost son than any of her contemporaries:

> They had to call and call
> And pick the worms off me like sticky pearls.
>
> Dying
> Is an art, like everything else.
> I do it exceptionally well.[42]

Like Roethke, Plath lost her father, Otto, at an early age
(she was nine), a catastrophic loss, as the early poem, "The
Colossus," attests ("I crawl like an ant in mourning"). The
later poetry in her two best-known volumes, *The Colossus*
(1960) and *Ariel* (1965), tries to account for this loss through
a significant number of poems in which the father-figure is
essentially portrayed as a love-hate object, sometimes sur-
facing as the male protagonist in an Electra theme ("The
Colossus," "Full Fathom Five," "The Beekeeper's Daughter," "Daddy"), sometimes in more equivocal terms as a
figure for contempt ("Man in Black," "Lady Lazarus,"
"Berck-Plage," "Strings," "The Hanging Man," "Little
Fugue," "Years,"). The ambivalent feeling Plath holds toward her father throughout her poetry manifests itself on
another, perhaps more profound level, and that is her own
sense of identity that is always on the edge—between life
and death. It is a Roethkean ambivalence really, dramatized
in the long poems as has been seen, and in Plath's particular
mode this ambivalence gives way, as it does for Roethke's
old woman at the end of her "Meditations," to the stasis of
perfection but without vision: "Perfection is terrible, it cannot have children./ Cold as snow breath, it tamps the
womb."[43] The penultimate poem in *Ariel*, "Edge," best describes this perfected condition:

> The woman is perfected.
> Her dead
>
> Body wears the smile of accomplishment,
> The illusion of a Greek necessity
>
> Flows in the scrolls of her toga,
> Her bare
>
> Feet seem to be saying:
> We have come so far, it is over.

But going back to *The Colossus* one sees where Plath developed from Roethke and how she was to extend his mode of identity through the dying of the self and ultimately distinguish herself poetically from the master.

Ted Hughes writes that Plath began reading Roethke "closely and sympathetically for the first time" while both of them were at Yaddo in the autumn of 1959, and that the series ending *The Colossus*, "Poem for a Birthday," is the result—Hughes goes on to describe it as

> "A series of pieces, each a monologue of some character in an underground, primitive drama. "Stones" was the last of them, and the only one not obviously influenced by Roethke. It is full of specific details of her experience in a mental hospital, and is clearly the first eruption of the voice that produced *Ariel*."[44]

In effect, Hughes is saying that Roethke is behind the voice that produced *Ariel*, Plath's most acclaimed work. Here in the "Birthday" series—which bears a strong resemblance to the structure of "The Lost Son" with its sequence of seven titled poems—just about every line is consciously Roethkean, cataloguing as they do the small shapes, sounds, and smells in a kingdom of bang and blab:

> Pebble smells, turnipy chambers.
> Small nostrils are breathing.
> Little humble loves!
> Footlings, boneless as noses,
> It is warm and tolerable
> In the bowel of the root.
> Here's a cuddly mother.

In the "Maenad" piece from this series, Plath records her particular trauma in Roethkean terms of regression, a trauma that undoubtedly shaped her poetry:

> Once I was ordinary:
> Sat by my father's bean tree
> Eating the fingers of wisdom.
> The birds made milk.
> When it thundered I hid under a flat stone.
>
> The mouther of mouths didn't love me.
> The old man shrank to a doll.
> O I am too big to go backward:
> Birdmilk is feathers,
> The bean leaves are dumb as hands.

The childlike utterances echoing the nursery rhythms from Roethke's *Praise to the End!* sequence, and particularly the opening section of "The Lost Son," dramatize the sudden separation from parents as one reads from the first to the second stanza. The absence of love from the living parent and the presence of death in the other fail to force the desired regression ("O I am too big to go backward"), as if Plath here has expressly taken exception to Roethke's lost son character. The last two lines are almost prophetic in telling that the vegetable and animal worlds will not come to her aid to help her shape an identity for herself, as they do for Roethke—particularly within the regenerative rhythms of "North American Sequence." No snail glisters her forward, no bird soft-sighs her home, and no roses keep breathing for her in the dark. Yet in the last piece, "The Stones," her characteristic ambivalence presents itself as she does return to the womb, "The wordless cupboard," to become remade, not from a world of nature, but from the hospital, "the city of spare parts":

> Love is the uniform of my bald nurse.
>
> Love is the bone and sinew of my curse.
> The vase, reconstructed, houses
> The elusive rose.

Ten fingers shape a bowl for shadows.
My mendings itch. There is nothing to do.
I shall be good as new.

"Poem for a Birthday" ends on this optimistic, yet tentative
note. Like Roethke's old woman character ("Love is my
wound"),[45] Plath, too, sees love as her undoing, a theme that
comes to define many of the *Ariel* poems, and expressed
here in terms of an alter ego, yet another theme running
through the later poetry. Plath sees herself here as the
reconstructed vase, pieced together, rather than reborn, in
which her "mendings itch" and the rose, symbol of a Roethkean order in nature (the greenhouse and the far field),
remains "elusive"—throughout her poetry.

When she was at Yaddo, Plath also wrote "Blue Moles,"
another poem written in the Roethkean mode and emphasizing, in particular, the animism in "The Lost Son":

Who stunned the dirt into noise?
                    Ask the mole, he knows.
I feel the slime of a wet nest.
                    Beware Mother Mildew.
Nibble again, fish nerves,

or even that of the old woman at the end of her "Meditations": "I'm wet with another life." Yet in Plath's case, the
animism takes the deathward direction (death of entire self)
that Roethke warns his speaker to be "Beware" of—the self
becomes mildewed, if only because Plath's creatures are
dead to begin with ("Moles dead in the pebbled rut"):

I enter the soft pelt of the mole.
Light's deaf to them: they shrivel in it.
They move through their mute rooms while I sleep,
Palming the earth aside, grubbers

After the fat children of root and rock.
By day, only the topsoil heaves.
Down there one is alone.

Again, note the Roethkean paradigm: unmasked speaker, present tense accenting the animism, and intuitive imagery ("grubbers/ After the fat children").

In the same year she attended Yaddo, Plath began her sequence of bee poems that accumulated to six in number; the first, "The Beekeeper's Daughter," appearing in *The Colossus*, and the remainder in *Ariel*. The beehive is an important symbol for Plath, as the greenhouse is for Roethke, because of its autobiographical and archetypal significance; it symbolizes, on the one hand, her early relationship with her father, who was a biology professor at Boston University and an authority on bumblebees, hence the beekeeper in her life (as Roethke's father might be called the keeper of flowers), and, on the other hand, the queen bee secreting the royal jelly ("The blood jet is poetry,/ There is no stopping it"[46]) doomed to die in a society of drones and "unmiraculous women,/ Honey-drudgers."[47]

Whereas Roethke's greenhouse is primarily a symbol of life—the exceptions perhaps best exemplified by the old woman's words at the end of her "Meditations": "I no longer cry for green in the midst of cinders,/ Or dream of the dead, and their holes"—Plath's beehive is a symbol of death, taking its cue, as it were, from Roethke's exceptions:

This is the room I have never been in.
This is the room I could never breathe in.
The black bunched in there like a bat,
No light
But the torch and its faint

Chinese yellow on appalling objects—
Black assinity. Decay.
Possession.
It is they who own me.[48]

But in the first of the bee poems the symbol is one of life, and the father, "maestro of the bees," is no different from Roethke's Papa, symbol of creation and order:

> A garden of mouthings. Purple, scarlet-speckled, black
> The great corollas dilate, peeling back their silks.
> Their musk encroaches, circle after circle,
> A well of scents almost too dense to breath in.
> Hieratical in your frock coat, maestro of the bees,
> You move among the many breasted hives.[49]

Like many of her contemporaries, Plath's poetry exemplifies and extends the Roethkean sense of ambivalence arising out of the search for identity in modern times, involving the self-destroying dangers of animism, of becoming wholly other, that the journey out of the self requires. In Roethke's poetry it was seen how this ambivalence eventually manifested itself in a regenerative way, that is, the ambivalence between self and nonself, or other, was eventually replaced by the regenerative patterns the poet envisioned in nature—patterns that developed through the long poems. The poetry is therapy for the poet (and for the reader), that is, the poetry must eventually satisfy the poet's own sense of identity within the world. Plath's ambivalence, however, never approaches the regenerative stage. Except for a few beginnings in *The Colossus*—the Roethkean poems, for example—the regenerative mode falls off as the ambivalence itself becomes more crystallized and schizophrenic:

> The still waters
> Wrap my lips,
>
> Eyes, nose and ears,
> A clear
> Cellophane I cannot crack.[50]

There is no half-way house for Plath as there is for Roethke, at least not a greenhouse where both the self and the other can take root; there is only the death house, the beehive, which, in nature, is more apt to be Plath's coffin: "Whose is that long white box in the grove, what have they accomplished, why am I cold?"[51] Most of the poems in *Ariel* dramatize a failure of the self to reach out to the other, to envisage nature other than something hostile, like the first section of "The Lost Son," or when Roethke's old woman is in the throes of despair. This failure can be softly expressed as when Plath speaks about her child in "Morning Song":

> All night your moth-breath
> Flickers among the flat pink roses. I wake to listen:
> A far sea moves in my ear,

or again using a Roethkean image in a stronger, more threatening sense, as in "Sheep in Fog":

> All morning the
> Morning has been blackening,
>
> A flower left out.
> My bones hold a stillness, the far
> Fields melt my heart.

They threaten
To let me through to a heaven
Starless and fatherless, a dark water,

and finally the cry of alienation amidst a sea of flowers in "Poppies in October":

O my God, what am I
That these late mouths should cry open
In a forest of frost, in a dawn of cornflowers.

In following Roethke, Plath, too, is drawn to the vegetable and floral realm of nature, much more than she is to the animal in nature, and, as has been seen, she continually risks her identity in claiming its power over her (*see*, for example, "Tulips," "Elm," "The Bee Meeting," "Little Fugue," "Poppies in July"). Only rarely does the floral world support her identity in the spirit of mergence, and even in the following example from "Fever 103°," identity is conditioned by physical illness:

Does not my heart astound you. And my light.
All by myself I am a huge camellia
Glowing and coming and going, flush on flush.

The sense of intense fear in Plath's poetry is symptomatic of the modern condition imposing its invidious technology on each new member of society, and to this extent Plath continually echoes Roethke's fear of the institution and those destructive potentialities it possesses: "In my sleeveless summery dress I have no protection,/ And they are all gloved and covered, why did nobody tell me?"[52] In her journey out of the self, Plath comes to the recognition that there are no pursuing forms, "no more idols," only the "absolute sacrifice" of herself, the *I* split now into, "Me and you," and into the stiffening shapes of "The Munich Mannequins":

> Perfection is terrible, it cannot have children.
> Cold as snow, it tamps the womb
>
> Where the yew trees blow like hydras,
> The tree of life and the tree of life
>
> Unloosing their moons, month after month, to no
>   purpose.
> The blood flood is the flood of love,
>
> The absolute sacrifice.
> It means: no more idols but me,
>
> Me and you.
> So, in their sulphur loveliness, in their smiles
>
> These mannequins lean tonight
> In Munich, morgue between Paris and Rome.

If Plath invokes the floral in nature to image a poetry that is essentially nihilistic, Ted Hughes invokes the animal in nature to image the nihilistic. Both poets represent complementary approaches to essentially similar themes, although Hughes shows a wider range of expression as well as an ability to engage the regenerative theme as a check to his nihilism, just as it provides a check to Roethke's mysticism.

The journey pattern so pervasive in Roethke's poetry reappears in Hughes's poetry—from *The Hawk in the Rain* (1956) to *Crow* (1970)—as a regressive theme back to a primitive state, often expressed as a Roethkean sense of nothingness ("Out of these nothings/—All beginnings come"), a void, or a hole ("dream of the dead, and their holes"), from which Hughes means to go forward, to fashion some sense of progress. There is a revealing children's poem from Hughes's "Meet My Folks" (like Roethke, Hughes can carry his primitivism into children's poems) that perhaps states as clearly as anywhere Hughes's purpose:

> A tentacle came groping from a hole that belonged to a
> mouse,
> A floor collapsed and Chinamen swarmed up into the
> house.
> A Hole's an unpredictable thing—
> Nobody knows what a Hole might bring.
> Caves in the mountain, clefts in the wall,
> My Father has to inspect them all![53]

Hole, void, or unconscious, this is the ground of beginning for so much of Hughes's poetry. Ideology is ignored, or transformed:

> Adam ate the apple.
> Eve ate Adam.
> The serpent ate Eve.
> This is the dark intestine,[54]

and about the only ritual left for Hughes to accept—because "Truth Kills Everybody"[55]—is blood sacrifice:

> *And still he who never has been killed*
> *Croaks helplessly*
> *And is only just born,*[56]

a theme that ends his first two volumes, *The Hawk in the Rain* and *Lupercal* (1960), and continues into *Crow*. Death is the way of redemption in the Roethkean sense of returning to a raw, primitive existence with nature. When W. D. Snod-

grass says that Hughes often does the same thing as
Roethke, only better, he surely is referring to the power of
Hughes's animal imagery, like "Pike," which, compared to
Roethke's "The Pike," is a closer description of these, "Killers from the egg"[57] and their habitat. Yet Hughes ends the
poem in what I have come to term the Roethkean mode; the
speaker, the rhythms, the imagery come together in these
lines to create the animistic sense of merging with nature:

<blockquote>

                                        It held
Pike too immense to stir, so immense and old
That past nightfall I dared not cast

But silently cast and fished
With the hair frozen on my head
For what might move, for what eye might move.
The still splashes on the dark pond,

Owls hushing the floating woods
Frail on my ear against the dream
Darkness beneath night's darkness had freed,
That rose slowly towards me, watching.

</blockquote>

But Hughes's poetry does not as a whole follow the
paradigm of Roethke's mode of identity, he moves on to
perfect his own voice. There are variations, for example,
when Hughes drops the *I* in favor of a mask

<blockquote>

                        (. . . lest they choose his head
Under severe moons he sits making
Wolf masks, mouths clamped well on to the world[58]),

</blockquote>

like "Hawk Roosting" from *Lupercal*, and extending then
this point of view into *Recklings* (1966), where he dramatizes
the transformation from *I* to other (bird) in the poem,
"Memory":

Claws trickle onto my palm.
An ounce pins itself there,

Nose wavering to investigate me.
Am I a mouse's remembrance?

I start, and it bounces past its shadow
Into my mother's shoe

Which twists out.
                    I fly up flustered
Into the winter of a near elm.

Giving the other a voice is developed to a greater extent in
Wodwo (1967), with such poems as "Mountains," "Gog,"
"Karma," "Song of a Rat," and "Wodwo," and, of course,
this point of view culminates in *Crow*, where Hughes gives
his bird-persona a speaking voice—dramatizing, too, what
Roethke had stated in "The Lost Son":

The weeds whined,
The snakes cried,
The cows and briars
Said to me: Die.

Hughes manages the omniscient voice for the most part,
especially in those poems where the description of the
other, the animal itself, like Roethke's crab and salmon
descriptions in "Meditations of an Old Woman," is indulged
in for its own sake; and for that reason the other in nature is
made sacred to the poet, like "Second Glance at a Jaguar,"
"The Howling of Wolves," and "Gnat-Psalm," where, in
fact, the *I* does reenter the poem to heighten the sense of
animistic merging:

O little Hasids
Ridden to death by your own bodies
Riding your bodies to death
You are the angels of the only heaven!

And God is an Almighty Gnat!
You are the greatest of all the galaxies!
My hands fly in the air, they are follies
My tongue hangs up in the leaves
My thoughts have crept into crannies

Your dancing

Your dancing

Rolls my staring skull slowly away into outer space.

Here is perhaps a good example of the animistic sense
degenerating into stasis; a death-wish really, death of the
self that shares with the death of the insect:

Their little bearded faces
Weaving and bobbing on the nothing
Shaken in the air, shaken, shaken
And their feet dangling like the feet of victims.

The pattern has been seen many times in Roethke's long
poems:

I sway outside myself
Into the darkening currents,
Into the small spillage of driftwood.

But one also finds in Hughes those regenerative patterns,
the animistic developing as a life force from a sense of stasis
or nothingness:

> I seem
> separate from the ground and not rooted but dropped
> out of nothing casually I've no threads
> fastening me to anything I can go anywhere
> I seem to have been given the freedom
> of this place what am I then?[59]

When the poet's animism takes this turn into the regenerative, he is, of course, invoking the metonymic trope, for the emphasis is on the action to be described in terms of motion and material with no seeming reference to a concept, or concepts, or any ideology, as he says in these lines:

> And the incomprehensible cry
> From the boughs, in the wind
> Sets us listening for below words,
> Meanings that will not part from the rock,[60]

that is perhaps best exemplified poetically in these lines:

> the head dragging forward, the body keeping up
> The hind legs lagging. He coils, he flourishes
> The blackjack tail as if looking for a target,
> Hurrying through the underworld, soundless.[61]

Certainly, Hughes, like Roethke, is in reaction to his times, to the immense pressures from an institutionalized society; that he finds himself forced by the extremes of violence that lays so much to waste—the pollution caused by human greed—to create in turn a sense of beginning from that nothingness and waste. Where the excesses of human behavior in society, the excesses of the self-involved, engendered in Roethke's poetry an opposing excessive zeal in the search for identity and ultimately mystical ecstasy ("I embrace the waters of the world"), these same conditions engender in much of Hughes's poetry an excessive zeal for nihilism, like "Truth Kills Everybody" from *Crow* where Crow (Hughes's mask) tenaciously pursues the protean forms of truth—doctrinal ideologies from the heoric concept embodied by Achilles to that of love embodied by Christ—until the violence generated by that pursuit results in Crow's annihilation ("He was blasted to nothing"). But Hughes manages to avoid these excesses, which in themselves are variants of a death-wish for the self, by engaging regenerative themes where the language takes a metonymic direction away from concept and abstraction back into the beginning world of process. In this way the ideal is shaped by the real, as seen in Roethke's long poems, particularly "North American Sequence." The regenerative patterns, suggesting a spirit hunting for form—literally, a shaping spirit—are hostile to concepts such as love, beauty, God, devil, and so on, and it is unimportant whether one imposes upon these verbal patterns preconceived notions about oneself, or society, for any imposition of this kind would have the effect of negating, or at least detracting from the sense of innocence and beginning inherent in the poetry itself. Hughes offers a good example of this kind of poetry, which perhaps embodies the paragon of the Roethkean mode, in "Stealing Trout on a May Morning" from *Recklings*. The poem is just over a hundred lines and approximates in structure any one of the poems making up one of Roethke's long sequences. Here again the unmasked *I* emerges, together with an accumulating sense of rhythm and imagery, defining a metonymic direction for language to take:

> I emerge. The air, after all, has forgotten everything.
> The sugared spindles and wings of grass
> Are etched on great goblets. A pigeon falls into space.

The earth is coming quietly and darkly up from a great
      depth,
Still under the surface. I am unknown,
But nothing is surprised. The tarmac of the road
Is velvet with sleep, the hills are out cold.
A new earth still in its wrapper
Of gauze and cellophane,
The frost from the storage still on its edges,
My privilege to poke and sniff.
The sheep are not much more than primroses.
And the river there, amazed with itself,
Flexing and trying its lights
And unused fish, that are rising
And sinking for the sheer novelty
As the sun melts the hill's spine and the spilled light
Flows through their gills . . . .

The regenerative pattern running through much of
Hughes's poetry makes an appeal for a sense of perma-
nence in life through mere repetition, where "the sun/ Rises
upon a world well-tried and old,"[62] where progress, like
Roethke's long poems, is not building a new Jerusalem in
England or America, but is in the "push of Adam's blood"
through the "agony"[63] of living and dying, or as seen
through the hawk's eyes:

The sun is behind me.
Nothing has changed since I began
My eye has permitted no change.
I am going to keep things like this,[64]

or through the eyes of Roethke's old woman: "By swoops of
bird, by leaps of fish, I live."
Yet there is the question of Hughes's increasing depen-
dence upon a mask for his voice, and here he swerves from
Roethke as much as Wright does for the opposite reason—

that of intensifying the unmasked voice, the autobiographical *I*. Whether the bird-mask that Hughes adopts in his last volume is effective and integral to his entire canon is difficult to say at this time. Presently, *Crow* seems to be a kind of third or fourth act in a developing Shakespearean tragedy—more like the mad scenes in *King Lear*, except Lear becomes unmasked, dethroned, and naked in the eye of nature's storm, whereas Hughes becomes lost, trying to hide in the darkness of that storm he re-creates. Perhaps in time this may prove to be better for the poetry; perhaps there has been too much emphasis placed on the *I* of the poet, the Romantic *I* that demands irrevocably a commitment to vision that the contemporary poet finds increasingly difficult to secure or even pursue in a culture that demands less and less from the individual. Rather than risk failure at attempting the prophetic voice, the poet today might find that a detached view of the world is more acceptable to the reader. It seems to me, however, that the good poet not only transcends the failures a neoromantic with a lesser talent is prey to, but he also helps to establish a readership at the broader based, precritical level, a following to put it simply, that is fundamental to the life of any art form. Hughes has his following, certainly, and it was well established before the publication of *Crow*; at any rate, the last poem in *Crow* may be pointing ahead to what is to come. The mask is partially dropped, and the spirit of small creatures is invoked:

> O littleblood, little boneless little skinless
> Ploughing with a linnet's carcase
> Reaping the wind and threshing the stones.

As neoromantics extending the Roethkean mode, these five writers might be viewed as personalities first and craftsmen or technicians second: Promethean writers, whom Denis Donoghue has described as those who refuse to accept the limits of language in determining their feeling, those writers who "drive the language."[65] Donoghue suggests that it is the charisma of such writers that attracts readers to them, and one often finds one has left his literary criticism behind, if only because it may prove embarrassing in showing appreciation. In the case of a Promethean figure like Roethke this *a* critical response must be given its due as readers become engaged in the risks—the risks of language—the poet takes in his journey, engaging, too, one's inner responsibilities with the poet to try to re-create the bounds of art and life. Like Yeats's long-legged fly upon the stream, the critic's mind, as well, must often move upon silence (and the delicate, articulated structure of Yeats's symbol reminds one even more of the immediacy, the reality, of those risks).

If Roethke dramatizes that edge between identity and nonidentity in his journey out of the self, then does he not reveal that it is still a viable area worth defining, that the modern poet must seek out his own locus of definition, his own particular edge, if his art is to survive? If the poet fails in this respect, is it not because he can no longer see the edge of his identity, that it no longer has meaning, either for the individual or the culture in which he lives?

Of the five poets here discussed, it seems Dickey is the most fragmentary; if there is vision in his work, it is not of the Blakean kind that insists on edge and outline, rather it is a vision parading personality—promoting, therefore, a poetry that is more diffuse than definitive. Bly, in his more recent poetry, seems to be impatient with the demands for a Roethkean mode; he is unwilling to continue to define an edge for himself and has instead been more concerned with appeasing his rhetorical talents. Plath most certainly defines an edge for herself by "driving the language" in the Roethkean sense, and she is interesting because she is perhaps the most Promethean of these five poets, having consciously destroyed that edge by stealing the fire from her own life. The edge of identity is almost annihilated in Hughes's last volume, *Crow*; whether there will be a resurgence of identity, a regeneration, remains to be seen. Wright is a poet who is willing to face his "inner responsibilities"—and whose latest volume, *Two Citizens*, is compelling in its willingness to understand his American identity.

Like every age, there is a plethora of bad poetry to go along with the good, and, as always, the distinction between the two involves not only questions of craft but a moral question as well—what Auden considered an individual's moral commitment to the language—a commitment of great importance for Roethke, who was aware of its all too noticeable absence:

> The trouble probably lies in the age itself, in the unwillingness of poets to face their ultimate inner responsibilities, in their willingness to seek refuge in words rather than transcending them. The language dictates; they are the used. The cohabitation of their images is, as it were, a mere fornication of residues.
>
> One can say that the poetry of the future will not come from such as these. Instead, it will be, let us hope, highly conscious, subtle and aware, yet not laboriously referential; eloquent but not heavily rhetorical; clear perhaps in the way Dantë is clear; sensuous but not simple minded; above all, rooted deeply in life; passionate and perhaps even suffused, on occasion, with wisdom and light.
>
> —(*SP*, 123, 124)

Here Roethke sums up the better qualities of poetry, of Milton's legacy really, that good poetry is simple, sensuous, and passionate. By adding that the poetry of the future, above all, should be rooted deeply in life, he invokes, too, the spirit of the deep image; and, of course, one is reminded of the sometimes tragic direction the Promethean plunge takes in its attempt to define an edge to human existence. The one reference to Dantë shows, I think, Roethke's roots in the long poem, or at least his concern for it; perhaps, too, his hope for its survival. Through Roethke's poetry, the Dantean experience is reborn, and to make this possible is Roethke's lasting contribution to American letters.

Notes

1. David Ossman, *The Sullen Art: Interviews with Modern American Poets* (New York: Corinth Books, 1963), pp. 27, 30, 34, 40.
2. *The Dyer's Hand and Other Essays* (New York: Random House, 1962), p. 367.
3. Since this chapter has gone to press, there has appeared a study along similar lines to mine by Anthony Libby, "Roethke, Water Father," *American Literature* 46 (November 1974): 267-88, that I note with enthusiasm. Although Professor Libby's method is less extensive than mine, concentrating mostly on Plath and Dickey, and drawing some different conclusions—less controversial perhaps—he does bring into necessary focus the question of Roethke's influence.
4. *Collected Poems* (Middletown, Connecticut: Wesleyan University Press, 1971). References to Wright's poetry from this edition will be indicated in the text by *WCP* and page number. As of this writing there has appeared a new volume of verse by Wright, *Two Citizens* (New York: Farrar, Straus and Giroux, 1973), which will not be discussed by me, since I feel my arguments for a Roethkean influence on Wright have been sufficiently structured by means of the collected poems.
5. *The Glass House*, pp. 56-58.
6. *Autobiographies* (London: MacMillan, 1955), p. 189.
7. "On English and American Poetry," *The Fifties* 2 (1959): 47.
8. "Five Decades of Modern American Poetry," *The Fifties* 1 (1958): 39.
9. "Some Notes on French Poetry," *The Sixties* 5 (Fall 1961): 70.
10. *Forty Poems Touching on Recent American Poetry* (Boston: Beacon Press, 1970), p. 11. See also, "The Work of James Wright," *The Sixties* 8 (Spring 1966: 77.
11. *See also*, "The Work of James Wright," *The Sixties* 8 (Spring 1966): 77.
12. *Forty Poems*, p. 15.
13. *Letters*, p. 142.
14. *Sleepers Joining Hands* (New York: Harper and Row, 1973), pp. 49, 50.
15. *Sleepers*, p. 62.
16. *Sleepers*, pp. 64, 65.

17. "Some Notes on French Poetry," p. 69.
18. *Sleepers*, p. 56.
19. One thinks of Matthew Arnold in connection with these titles, Arnold having left off his poetry for criticism in order to structure his despairing themes about society. It seems, however, that American poets (Eliot, Pound, Crane, Roethke) had taken up with their poetry where Arnold had left off, and as Eliot has said: "The vision of the horror and the glory was denied to Arnold, but he knew something of the boredom," *The Use of Poetry and the Use of Criticism* (London: Faber and Faber, 1933), p. 106.
20. *The Light Around the Body* (New York: Harper and Row, 1967), p. 14.
21. *The Light*, p. 13.
22. *The Light*, p. 44.
23. *The Light*, p. 62.
24. *Silence in the Snowy Fields* (Middletown, Connecticut: Wesleyan University Press, 1962), p. 26.
25. *Silence*, p. 20.
26. *Silence*, p. 31.
27. *Silence*, p. 37.
28. *Silence*, p. 53.
29. *Forty Poems*, p. 17.
30. *Sorties: Journals and New Essays* (Garden City, New York: Doubleday, 1971), p. 204.
31. Dickey has this to say about Bly and Wright: "fanciful only," "derivative, imitative . . .unimaginative" (*Sorties*, pp. 102, 198); about Hughes: "Just read Ted Hughes's *Crow*. That's the kind of stuff I throw away," "self-conscious primitivism" (*Sorties*, pp. 105, 118); about Plath: "poetry of the hysterical intelligence," "bad—awful," "slick," "solipsistic" (*Sorties*, pp. 67, 69, 191).
32. *Sorties*, p. 101.
33. *Sorties*, p. 161.
34. *James Dickey Poems 1957-1967* (Middletown, Connecticut: Wesleyan University Press, 1967), p. 60. References to Dickey's poems from this edition will be indicated in the text by *DCP* and number.
35. *Self-Interviews* (Garden City, New York: Doubleday, 1970), p. 89.
36. *Sorties*, p. 88.
37. *Sorties*, p. 53.
38. *Sorties*, pp. 107, 108.
39. *Sorties*, p. 58.
40. *Sorties*, p. 96.
41. *The Eye-Beaters, Blood, Victory, Madness, Buckhead, and Others* (Garden City, New York: Doubleday, 1970), p. 46.
42. *Ariel* (New York: Harper and Row, 1965), p. 7.
43. *Ariel*, p. 73.
44. *The Art of Sylvia Plath*, p. 192.

45. A tragic notion of love, as in these lines from "Her Becoming":

What lover keeps his song?
I sigh before I sing.
I love because I am
A rapt thing with a name.

46. *Ariel*, p. 82.
47. *Ariel*, p. 61.
48. *Ariel*, p. 67.
49. *The Colossus* (London: Faber and Faber, 1967), p. 75.
50. *Ariel*, p. 78.
51. *Ariel*, p. 58.
52. *Ariel*, p. 56.
53. *Poetry Is* (Garden City, New York: Doubleday, 1970), p. 89.
54. *Wodwo* (London: Faber and Faber, 1967), p. 149.
55. *Crow* (New York: Harper and Row, 1970), p. 71.
56. *Crow*, p. 72.
57. *Lupercal* (New York: Harper and Bros., 1960), p. 56. *See Also*, "W. D. Snodgrass: An Interview," *Salmagundi*, no. 22-23 (Spring/Summer 1973), p. 154.
58. *Lupercal*, p. 13.
59. *Wodwo*, p. 183.
60. *Wodwo*, p. 29.
61. *Wodwo*, pp. 25, 26.
62. *Recklings* (London: Turret Books, 1966), p. 34.
63. *Crow*, p.75.
64. *Lupercal*, p. 26.
65. *Thieves of Fire* (London: Faber & Faber, 1973), p. 24.

Selected Bibliography

Works and Materials by Theodore Roethke

Collected Poems of Theodore Roethke, The. Garden City, New York: Doubleday, 1966.

On the Poet and His Craft: Selected Prose of Theodore Roethke. Edited by Ralph J. Mills, Jr., Seattle: University of Washington Press, 1965.

Selected Letters of Theodore Roethke. Edited by Ralph J. Mills, Jr., Seattle: University of Washington Press, 1968.

Straw for the Fire: From the Notebooks of Theodore Roethke, (1943-1963). Edited by David Wagoner. New York: Doubleday, 1972.

Related Works

Articles

Abrams, M. H. "Structure and Style in the Greater Romantic Lyric." In *Romanticism and Consciousness: Essays in Criticism,* edited by Harold Bloom, pp. 201-232. New York: W. W. Norton & Co., 1970.

Berryman, John. "From the Middle and Senior Generations." *American Scholar* 28 (Summer 1959): 384-90.

Bly, Robert. "Five Decades of Modern American Poetry." *The Fifties* 1 (1958): 36-39.

————. "On English and American Poetry." *The Fifties* 2 (1959): 45-47.

————. "Some Notes on French Poetry." *The Sixties* 5 (Fall 1961): 66-70.

————. "The Work of James Wright." *The Sixties* 8 (Spring 1966): 52-78.

Burke, Kenneth. "The Vegetal Radicalism of Theodore Roethke." *Sewanee Review* 58 (Winter 1950): 68-108. Reprinted in *Profile of Theodore Roethke*, editor, William Heyen, pp. 19-46. Columbus, Ohio: Charles E. Merrill Co., 1971.

Dickey, James. "The Greatest American Poet." *Atlantic* 222 (November 1968): 53-58. Reprinted in *Sorties: Journals and New Essays*, pp. 214-24. Edited by James Dickey, Garden City, New York: Doubleday, 1971.

Donoghue, Denis. "Theodore Roethke." In *Connoisseurs of Chaos: Ideas of Order in Modern American Poetry*, pp. 216-45. New York: Macmillan, 1965. Reprinted as "Roethke's Broken Music," in *Theodore Roethke: Essays on the Poetry*, edited by Arnold Stein, pp. 136-66. Seattle: University of Washington Press, 1965.

Fiedler, Leslie A. "A Kind of Solution: The Situation of Poetry Now." *Kenyon Review* 26 (Winter 1964): 63-64.

Galvin, Brendan. "Theodore Roethke's Proverbs." *Concerning Poetry* 5 (Spring 1972): 35-47.

Hamilton, Ian. "Theodore Roethke." *Agenda* 3 (April 1964): 5-10.

Heyen, William. "The Divine Abyss: Theodore Roethke's Mysticism." *Texas Studies in Literature and Language* 11 (Winter 1969): 1,051-68. Reprinted in *Profile of Theodore Roethke*, edited by Heyen, pp. 100-116. Columbus, Ohio: Charles E. Merrill Co., 1971.

————. "Theodore Roethke's Minimals." *Minnesota Review* 8 (1968): 359-75.

Hoffman, Frederick J. "Theodore Roethke: The Poetic Shape of Death." In *Theodore Roethke: Essays on the Poetry*, edited by Arnold Stein, pp. 94-114. Seattle: University of

Washington Press, 1965. Reprinted in *Modern American Poetry: Essays in Criticism*, edited by Jerome Mazzaro, pp. 301-320. New York: McKay, 1970.

Kinnell, Galway. "To the Roots: An Interview with Galway Kinnell." *Salmagundi*, no. 22-23 (Spring/Summer 1973), pp. 206-221.

Kizer, Carolyn. "Poetry: School of the Pacific Northwest." *New Republic* 135 (16 July 1956): 18-19.

Kunitz, Stanley. "'Imagine Wrestling with an Angel': An Interview with Stanley Kunitz." *Salmagundi*, no. 22-23 (Spring/Summer 1973), pp. 71-83.

————. "Roethke: Poet of Transformations." *New Republic* 152 (23 January 1965): 23-29. Reprinted in *Profile of Theodore Roethke*, edited by William Heyen, pp. 67-77. Columbus, Ohio: Charles E. Merrill Co., 1971.

Lee, Charlotte, I. "The Line as a Rhythmic Unit in the Poetry of Theodore Roethke." *Speech Monographs* 30 (March 1963): 15-22.

Levi, Peter S. J. "Theodore Roethke." *Agenda* 3 (April 1964): 11-14.

Libby, Anthony. "Roethke, Water Father." *American Literature* 46 (November 1974): 267-88.

McMichael, James. "The Poetry of Theodore Roethke." *The Southern Review* 5 (Winter 1969): 4-25. Reprinted in *Profile of Theodore Roethke*, edited by William Heyen, pp. 78-95. Columbus, Ohio: Charles E. Merrill Co., 1971.

Martz, Louis L. "Recent Poetry: The Elegiac Mode." *Yale Review* 54 (Winter 1965): 285-98.

————. "Theodore Roethke: A Greenhouse Eden." In *The Poem of the Mind: Essays on Poetry/English and American*, pp. 162-82. New York: Oxford University Press, 1966. Reprinted as "A Greenhouse Eden," in *Theodore Roethke: Essays on the Poetry*, edited by Arnold Stein, pp. 14-35. Seattle: University of Washington Press, 1965.

Mazzaro, Jerome. "Theodore Roethke and the Failures of Language." *Modern Poetry Studies* 1 (July 1970): 73-96. Reprinted in *Profile of Theodore Roethke*, edited by William Heyen, pp. 47-64. Columbus, Ohio: Charles E. Merrill Co., 1971.

Meredith, William. "A Steady Storm of Correspondences: Theodore Roethke's Long Journey Out of the Self." *Shenandoah* 16 (Autumn 1964): 41-54. Reprinted in *Theodore Roethke: Essays on the Poetry*, edited by Arnold Stein, pp. 36-53. Seattle: University of Washington Press, 1965.

Mills, Ralph J., Jr. "In the Way of Becoming: Roethke's Last Poems." In *Theodore Roethke: Essays on the Poetry*, edited by Arnold Stein, pp. 115-35. Seattle: University of Washington Press, 1965.

————. "Theodore Roethke." In *Contemporary American Poetry*, pp. 48-71. New York: Random House, 1965.

————. "Theodore Roethke: The Lyric of the Self." In *Poets in Progress: Critical Prefaces to Ten Contemporary American Poets*, edited by Edward B. Hungerford, pp. 3-24. Evanston, Illinois: Northwestern University Press, 1962.

Nemerov, Howard. "Three in One." *Kenyon Review* 15 (Winter 1954): 148-54. Reprinted as "On Shapiro, Roethke, Winters," in *Poetry and Fiction: Essays*, edited by Nemerov, pp. 134-43. New Brunswick, New Jersey: Rutgers University Press, 1963.

Pearce, Roy Harvey. "Theodore Roethke: The Power of Sympathy." In *Theodore Roethke: Essays on the Poetry*, edited by Arnold Stein, pp. 167-99. Seattle: University of Washington Press, 1965. Reprinted in *Historicism Once More: Problems and Occasions for the American Scholar*, edited by Pearce, pp. 294-326. Princeton, New Jersey: Princeton University Press, 1969.

Pritchard, William H. "Wildness of Logic in Modern Lyric." In *Forms of Lyric*, edited by Reuben A. Brower, pp. 127-51. New York: Columbia University Press, 1970.

Ramsey, Jarold. "Roethke in the Greenhouse." *Western Humanities Review* 26 (Winter 1972): 35-47.

Schwartz, Delmore. "The Cunning and the Craft of the Unconscious and the Preconscious." *Poetry* 94 (June 1959):

203-205. Reprinted in *Selected Essays of Delmore Schwartz*, edited by Donald A. Dike and David H. Zucker, pp. 197-99. Chicago: University of Chicago Press, 1971; also in *Profile of Theodore Roethke*, edited by William Heyen, pp. 64-66. Columbus, Ohio: Charles E. Merrill Co., 1971.

Scott, Nathan A., Jr. "The Example of Roethke." In *The Wild Prayer of Longing and the Sacred*, edited by Scott, pp. 76-118. New Haven, Connecticut: Yale University Press, 1971.

Snodgrass, W. D. "'That Anguish of Concreteness'—Theodore Roethke's Career." In *Theodore Roethke: Essays on the Poetry*, edited by Arnold Stein, pp. 78-93. Seattle: University of Washington Press, 1965.

———. "W. D. Snodgrass: An Interview." *Salmagundi*, no. 22-23 (Spring/Summer 1973), pp. 149-63.

Spender, Stephen. "The Objective Ego." In *Theodore Roethke: Essays on the Poetry*, edited by Arnold Stein, pp. 3-13. Seattle: University of Washington Press, 1965.

Staples, Hugh B. "The Rose in the Sea-Wind: A Reading of Theodore Roethke's 'North American Sequence.'" *American Literature* 36 (May 1964): 189-203.

Tate, Allen. "In Memoriam—Theodore Roethke, 1908-1963." *Encounter* 21 (October 1963): 68.

Truesdale, C. W. "Theodore Roethke and the Landscape of American Poetry." *Minnesota Review* 8 (1968): 345-58.

Vernon, John. "Theodore Roethke's *Praise to the End!* Poems." *The Iowa Review* 2 (Fall 1971): 60-79.

Wain, John. "Theodore Roethke." *Critical Quarterly* 6 (Winter 1964): 322-28. Reprinted as "The Monocle of My Sea-Faced Uncle," in *Theodore Roethke: Essays on the Poetry*, edited by Arnold Stein, pp. 54-77. Seattle: University of Washington Press, 1965.

Wesling, Donald. "The Inevitable Ear: Freedom and Necessity in Lyric Form, Wordsworth and After." *Journal of English Literary History* 36 (1969): 544-61. Reprinted in *Forms of Lyric*, edited by Reuben A. Brower, pp. 103-126. New York: Columbia University Press, 1970.

Wilbur, Richard. "Poetry's Debt to Poetry." *Hudson Review* 26 (Summer 1973): 273-94.

Books

Abrams, M. H. *Natural Supernaturalism: Tradition and Revolution in Romantic Literature*. New York: W. W. Norton & Co., 1971.

Alvarez, A. *The Shaping Spirit: Studies in Modern English and American Poets*. London: Chatto and Windus, 1958.

Auden, W. H. *The Dyer's Hand and Other Essays*. New York: Random House, 1962.

———. *Forewords and Afterwords*. New York: Random House, 1973.

———. *Secondary Worlds*. London: Faber and Faber, 1968.

Blessing, Richard A. *Theodore Roethke's Dynamic Vision*. Bloomington, Indiana: Indiana University Press, 1974.

Bloom, Harold. *The Ringers in the Tower: Studies in Romantic Tradition*. Chicago: University of Chicago Press, 1971.

———, editor. *Romanticism and Consciousness: Essays in Criticism*. New York: W. W. Norton & Co., 1970.

Bly, Robert, ed. *Forty Poems Touching on Recent American Poetry*. Boston: Beacon Press, 1970.

Brereton, Geoffrey. *Principles of Tragedy: A Rational Examination of the Tragic Concept in Life and Literature*. Coral Gables, Florida: University of Miami Press, 1968.

Brower, Reuben A., ed. *Forms of Lyric*. New York: Columbia University Press, 1970.

Burke, Kenneth. *A Grammar of Motives*. Berkeley, California: University of California Press, 1969.

Dembo, L. S. *Conceptions of Reality in Modern American Poetry*. Berkeley, California: University of California Press, 1966.

Deutsch, Babette. *The Poetry in Our Time: A Critical Survey of Poetry in the English Speaking World, 1900-1960*. Garden City, New York: Doubleday, 1963.

Dickey, James. *Self-Interviews*. Garden City, New York: Doubleday, 1970.

———. *Sorties: Journals and New Essays*. Garden City, New York: Doubleday, 1971.

Dodsworth, Martin, ed. *The Survival of Poetry: A Contemporary Survey*. London: Faber and Faber, 1970.

Donoghue, Denis. *Connoisseurs of Chaos: Ideas of Order in Modern American Poetry*. New York: Macmillan, 1965.

———. *Thieves of Fire*. London: Faber and Faber, 1973.

Ehrenpreis, Irvin, et al., ed. *American Poetry: Stratford-Upon-Avon Studies 7*. New York: St. Martin's Press, 1965.

Eliot, T. S. *The Use of Poetry and the Use of Criticism*. London: Faber and Faber, 1933.

Gross, Harvey. *Sound and Form in Modern Poetry*. Ann Arbor, Michigan: University of Michigan Press, 1964.

Heyen, William, ed. *Profile of Theodore Roethke*. Columbus, Ohio: Charles E. Merrill Co., 1971.

McLeod, James R. *Theodore Roethke: A Bibliography*. Kent, Ohio: Kent State University Press, 1973.

Malkoff, Karl. *Theodore Roethke: An Introduction to the Poetry*. New York: Columbia University Press, 1966.

Martz, William J. *The Achievement of Theodore Roethke*. Glenview, Illinois: Scott, Foresman, 1966.

Mazzaro, Jerome, ed. *Modern American Poetry: Essays in Criticism*. New York: McKay, 1970.

Miller, J. Hillis. *Poets of Reality: Six Twentieth-Century Writers*. Cambridge, Massachusetts: Harvard University Press, 1965.

Mills, Ralph J., Jr. *Contemporary American Poetry*. New York: Random House, 1965.

———. *Theodore Roethke*. University of Minnesota Pamphlets on American Writers, no. 30. Minneapolis: University of Minnesota Press, 1963.

Nemerov, Howard. *Poetry and Fiction: Essays*. New Brunswick, New Jersey: Rutgers University Press, 1963.

Newman, Charles, ed. *The Art of Sylvia Plath*. Bloomington, Indiana: Indiana University Press, 1970.

Oates, Joyce Carol. *The Edge of Impossibility: Tragic Forms in Literature*. Greenwich, Connecticut: Fawcett, 1973.

Ossman, David. *The Sullen Art: Interviews with Modern American Poets*. New York: Corinth Books, 1963.

Ostroff, Anthony, editor. *The Contemporary Poet as Artist and Critic*. New York: Little, Brown, 1964.

Rosenthal, M. L. *The Modern Poets: A Critical Introduction*. New York: Oxford University Press, 1965.

———. *The New Poets: American and British Poets Since World War II*. New York: Oxford University Press, 1967.

Scott, Nathan A., Jr. *The Wild Prayer of Longing and the Sacred*. New Haven, Connecticut: Yale University Press, 1971.

Seager, Allan. *The Glass House: The Life of Theodore Roethke*. New York: McGraw-Hill Co., 1968.

Simpson, Louis. *An Introduction to Poetry*. 2nd edition. New York: St. Martin's Press, 1972.

Spears, Monroe K. *Dionysus and the City: Modernism in Twentieth-Century Poetry*. New York: Oxford University Press, 1970.

Stein, Arnold, ed. *Theodore Roethke: Essays on the Poetry*. Seattle, University of Washington Press, 1965.

Stepanchev, Stephen. *American Poetry Since 1945: A Critical Survey*. New York: Harper and Row, 1965.

Tate, Allen, ed. *Six American Poets: From Emily Dickinson to the Present: An Introduction*. Minneapolis: University of Minnesota Press, 1964.

Waggoner, Hyatt H. *American Poets: From the Puritans to the Present*. Boston: Houghton Mifflin, 1968.

Weatherhead, A. Kingsley. *The Edge of the Image: William Carlos Williams, Marianne Moore, and Some Other Poets*. Seattle: University of Washington Press, 1967.

Whitehead, Alfred North. *Science and the Modern World*. New York: Macmillan, 1925.

Williams, Raymond. *Modern Tragedy*. London: Chatto and Windus, 1969.

Yeats, W. B. *Autobiographies*. London: Macmillan, 1955.

———. *Essays and Introductions*. New York: Collier Books, 1968.

Poetry: A Short List

James Wright

> *The Green Wall* (1957); *Saint Judas* (1959); *The Branch Will Not Break* (1963); *Shall We Gather at the River* (1968); *Collected Poems* (1971); *Two Citizens* (1973).

Robert Bly

> *Silence in the Snowy Fields* (1962); *The Light Around the Body* (1967); *The Morning Glory* (1969); *Teeth Mother Naked at Last* (1970); *The Shadow Mothers* (1970); *Jumping Out of Bed* (1972); *Sleepers Joining Hands* (1973).

James Dickey

> *Into the Stone* (1957); *Drowing with Others* (1962); *Helmets* (1964); *Buckdancer's Choice* (1965); *Poems 1957-1967* (1967); *The Eye-Beaters, Blood, Victory, Madness, Buckhead, and Others* (1970); *Exchanges* (1971).

Sylvia Plath

> *The Colossus* (1962); *Ariel* (1965); *Crossing the Water* (1971); *The Winter Trees* (1971).

Ted Hughes

> *The Hawk in the Rain* (1957); *Lupercal* (1960); *Selected Poems* (1962); *Wodwo* (1967); *Recklings* (1967); *Poetry Is* (1970); *Crow* (1970).

Index

This study not only reveals the important contribution to poetry that Theodore Roethke provided, but also illuminates his effect on five major present-day poets—James Wright, Robert Bly, James Dickey, Sylvia Plath, Ted Hughes—who acknowledge Roethke's influence. By utilizing the critical analysis and biographical insights in the literature, Professor Williams compares five modern poets with their mentor and re-evaluates and examines the poetry loved by poets, written by the poet's poet. Throughout Roethke's life and even after his death, most poets have enthusiastically praised his work, while major critics have generally ignored or slighted him. What is particularly admirable in Roethke's poetry is his unusual intensity of the lyric voice, the projection of a preconscious self into the life of plants and animals, utilizing highly original free-verse patterns; as poet John Berryman describes it, "Teutonic, irregular, colloquial, delicate, botanical and psychological, irreligious, personal."